THE AUTHORIZED BIOGRAPHY OF
THE GREENES

America's Southern Gospel Trio

By Mike Collins
Foreword By Bill Gaither

Published In Beautiful West Virginia By Woodland Gospel Publishing House
A Division Of Woodland Press, LLC
www.woodlandgospel.com
SAN: 2 5 4 – 9 9 9 9

INTRODUCTION

"The Greenes are some of the sweetest people in Gospel music. It is rare that you find a group that isn't afraid to sing songs with powerful lyrics. I thank God for them and am honored that they have chosen to use many of my songs on their recordings. Most of all I am thankful for their integrity. A good name is above the price of rubies and the Greenes have held strongly to that!"

— Dottie Rambo

***

The Lord has blessed our ministry to cross paths with some of the best Christian workers in the nation. It has been an honor to minister along side of some of the "greats" in Southern Gospel Music. I bless the day the Lord brought The Greenes into our life. They have appeared regularly on our television and radio broadcasts which now reaches over 30 million people in America alone. They have sung in a large number of our camp meetings and crusades. I can honestly say there has never been a group to sing with more power and anointing than this group. They always put their whole heart into their ministry and the Lord uses them to prepare the hearts of the listeners to receive His Word.

It is one of the highlights of my ministry to be able to finally have an opportunity to share my love for this family. They started their ministry the same year that I began to preach the Gospel. We have been privileged to work together for most of those years. There are not adequate words in my vocabulary to express the gratitude I have for them. I thank them for blessing my heart time and time again with the gifts the Lord has granted unto them.

Now through this book, you too will have a chance to know more about these wonderful friends and you too can appreciate them for the ministry they have given to others.

To my friends, The Greenes, thanks for loving the Lord and living the life.

Stay Blessed in all you do.

By His Love,
Dr. Calvin Ray Evans

3

A young Tony and Tim Greene talk with Paul Heil in the 1980s.

I have been privileged to know the Greenes for many years. Even if you don't know them well now, you will know them after reading this outstanding biography of this very popular family singing group. You'll quickly learn that being a traveling Gospel singing group is not all glamour and excitement. This family has faced the same problems you and I face — including difficult health problems and disappointments. But you will be challenged and encouraged by their faith through trials and their excitement through victories as they share in song (and in words) what is most important to them — the Gospel message.

— **Paul Heil**, host of the nationally-syndicated "The Gospel Greats" radio program; operator (with his wife, Shelia) of Springside Marketing 1-800-38-MUSIC, a mail order marketing firm for Southern Gospel music.

DEDICATION

This book is dedicated to my lovely wife,
Jewell Collins, for having patience with me
during this project. I also dedicate it to the
devoted fans of this wonderful music we call
Southern Gospel.

"God is great, God is good, Even when we denied Him He stood. If no one could love us, He would. God is great, God is good."

— By Tim Greene,
"God Is Great," *The Cross*

FOREWORD

There are some people who believe that placing our faith in God somehow exempts us from pain and difficulty. And those same individuals eventually learn the truth ... that no one lives a challenge-free existence. The Greenes have expressed God's goodness far more dramatically than a pain-free life; their story demonstrates authentic trust and indescribable joy in the midst of suffering and hardship.

Through the pages of this book, Mike Collins reveals the challenges, health battles, grief and stress this beloved family has encountered during their extensive singing career. What you will discover is how this family kept going ... kept trusting ... and kept singing.

I'm more convinced than ever that the wonderful harmony you hear when this threesome sings is the evidence of far more than excellent vocal ability ... it is the result of a blending of spirits who have been bonded together by God's amazing grace.

The Greenes have proven time and time again that believers — even those who have given their lives to singing of God's faithfulness — face the same circumstances of life that everyone else does. But the hope and optimism they have found in Christ is a testimony to all of us who face dark days ... a testimony of victory through Jesus.

— Bill Gaither

TABLE OF CONTENTS

CHAPTER ONE
I AM A CHRISTIAN

"Next to the Word of God, music
deserves the highest praise. The gift
of language combined with the gift of
song was given to man that he should
proclaim the Word of God through
music."

— Martin Luther

The year was 1944. America had barely survived the Great Depression when she found herself thrust into a second world war against Japan and Nazi Germany and her allies. After several years of combat, battles and tragedy, America would claim victory within twelve months.

History reveals several major news events during that year: D-Day, the Battle of the Bulge and the liberation of many cities and countries previously seized by the enemy. The World Series was a one-city battle as the St. Louis Cardinals won the only St. Louis World Series in six games over the St. Louis Browns.

It was also the same year that six-year-old Everette Greene discovered something fascinating that would change his life forever. "I was listening to a girl play the piano in school," Everette recalls, "and I'll never forget thinking that it was the most beautiful sound I had ever heard."

His parents, Ralph and Tressie Greene, struggled to make ends meet, yet their dreams of a better life for their children never wavered. Ralph often worked away from home, leaving Tressie alone to care for the children, home and property. As a result, when Tressie went grocery shopping, Everette and his younger brother, John, would always tag along.

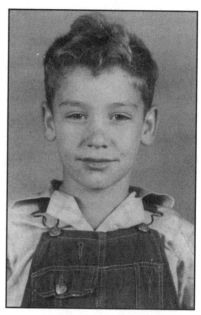

Everette Greene

Next door to the local schoolhouse in Baird's Creek, North Carolina, a small country store stood, serving as the heartbeat of the rural community. With groceries and other home necessities in the front and furniture in the back, the owner, Mr. Farthing, stocked his shelves with many items, but pianos were his specialty.

Everette often slipped away from his mother and sneaked into the backroom to explore the pianos on display. He would climb up onto a swivel stool and examine every inch of the ivory keyboard; with feet dangling half a foot or so from the pedals, his small fingers effortlessly picked out familiar tunes. He was especially fascinated with the differences between the white and black keys, and how the wooden hammers inside the piano would magically strike the wires as each key was played.

The young boy's talent soon captured the attention of Mr. Farthing, who shielded the youngster from his mother's scolding over touching the costly instruments. In fact, it was Mr. Farthing who suggested the couple buy a piano for Everette. But, of course, money was hard to come by in those days, and although Tressie wanted her son to have one, she knew they couldn't afford it.

Meanwhile, the young boy's interest in music grew with each

passing day. While his schoolmates ate lunch or romped around the playground playing tag or kickball, Everette would often make a beeline for the country store next door. Mr. Farthing would smile and nod as the excited young boy ran past the front counter to the piano room.

Mr. Farthing eventually told Tressie about Everette's daily practice visits, emphasizing the boy's need for a piano at home to rehearse more than just the few moments a day he could squeeze in at the store. At first Tressie thought the elderly storeowner was merely trying to make a sale, but soon realized he was only being honest. Although she had made it clear they could not afford a piano, the determined owner led Tressie to the pianos in the backroom.

"You see that one?" he asked, pointing out a small upright in the corner; "I'm going to sell you that piano for five dollars!"

Yet five dollars was still a lot of money in those days; Tressie already had to barter for her groceries and supplies with fresh eggs and other goods, as it was.

"Mr. Farthing, I can't pay for it," she said, as she looked to the floor and blushed from the embarrassment. "I don't know how in the world I could ever be able to come up with the money."

"You can pay for it anytime you want to and can," he said with a smile, "any way you want to and can. So, if it's just twenty-five or fifty cents at a time, that will be okay. Whatever it is, that child's got to have a piano."

Finally talking Tressie into the arrangement, he delivered the piano to the Greenes' small frame home that day and set it up in a corner of their living room. After Mr. Farthing left, Ralph voiced his concerns about paying for the instrument. Tressie waved her hands toward him as if to physically say "settle down, Ralph," and then explained that she didn't know how it would all work just yet, but somehow they would manage to pay for the used upright.

Ralph, Tressie and young Everette Greene singing together

And they eventually did, usually only a few cents at a time, until finally paying the bill in full — sometimes with fresh eggs and garden vegetables left over after buying the groceries and other supplies they needed. As it turns out, it was the best five dollars the couple had ever spent. On many evenings Everette played that piano from the time he returned home from school until his parents made him go to bed.

"We practically had to chase him away from that thing," Tressie remembers, grinning. "He wanted to stay on it constantly."

From plucking notes to learning how to create pleasing chords, little Everette's talent seemingly grew by the hour. With no formal lessons to speak of at this point, what young Everette accomplished during that first year was nothing short of astonishing.

Ralph and Tressie owned one of the first radios in their community, and before long young Everette was playing songs he'd heard on the daily Gospel broadcasts. Listening to the home radio kept him up on both the sacred classics and the latest hits. It was also common for the family to gather around the radio during the Saturday night Grand Ole Opry WSM program, broadcast from the old Ryman Auditorium in Nashville.

By the next year, Tressie, Ralph and Everette began performing in their home church as a trio. Amazingly, seven-year-old Everette played the piano not only for the family group, but he also began playing for the church's small country choir.

Everette took his playing so seriously, that while many children his age were outside playing baseball and other sports, he was inside "banging on that old piano," as he now says. He wanted to be the best he could be, and nothing would separate him from his dream. He spent many hours each day learning new chords and melodies, while searching for better ways to play. He also had an ear for recognizing and picking up new and unusual methods by other artists. Once he heard something innovative , he would then make it his goal to master the newly discovered technique and incorporate it into his own playing style.

Within several months, the family trio began performing for revival services, singing conventions, homecomings, and special performances in neighboring churches. Spectators expressed their amazement at the talent and sincerity young Everette displayed. The word quickly spread about this incredible little pianist, and crowds flocked to see him perform each night.

One Saturday the Greenes received an invitation to sing at the annual Rural Electrification Administration meeting in Lenoir, North Carolina. This would be the biggest event for the young family trio so far. Tressie and Ralph were a little leery of performing in front of such a large crowd, afraid of pushing their eight-year-old son too far, too fast. But it was Everette who did all the pushing — determined to perform in front of the "big crowd," he wouldn't let his parents talk him out of it.

The REA meeting was only the beginning of a busy schedule for the trio. The Greenes began singing in churches everywhere — including those in surrounding counties, cities and towns. In addition, the family traveled with several local pastors and evangelists throughout the tri-state area, ministering in revivals and special meetings.

During this time, Tressie decided that perhaps Everette should take conventional piano lessons, to hone his musical skills. She thought that if he had done so well with no one teaching him, then he would surely do wonders with proper lessons. However, there were no local piano teachers at the time, and Tressie wasn't even sure if they could afford the lessons, but she at least wanted to check into it.

There were two piano teachers in nearby Boone, and arrangements were made for Everette to begin taking lessons from a woman named Mrs. Tate. Although the lessons were a costly dollar each, Ralph and Tressie wanted their son to have the best training possible.

Everette's dissatisfaction became obvious after only a few lessons. Although Mrs. Tate was a wonderful teacher, Everette had already developed a rather polished style of his own and had little interest in learning a new way of playing.

After a couple of years of tutelage, Mrs. Tate finally told Tressie that in her opinion Everette would never benefit from her teaching. In fact, Mrs. Tate admitted that Everette's style was better than her own, and that she couldn't play as well as he could. As someone restricted to playing only whatever notes were written on the sheet music, she related how Everette was able to fill in the empty spots and give life to areas that were dead on paper.

Despite his disinterest, Everette did learn to read music, although he still preferred to play by ear. Performing only what notes were written on the sheet music was far too restrictive for the young boy's musical talents.

"The lessons never seemed to really sink in much," Everette recalls, "so I just continued on my own."

Everette briefly took lessons from another woman in Boone, but those lessons eventually ended as well, and for the same reason: the young boy simply had no use for them.

As the years passed, the Greenes' little home was constantly full of young people from the local church and neighborhood, who would gather around the piano singing and practicing Gospel songs up into the late hours of the night. Everette helped form several singing groups and quartets from these local talents.

By the time he was in high school, Everette formed singing groups with classmates as well. He and other students would perform for their peers and neighboring church members. There was no doubt Everette loved to perform. He was constantly singing, booking nearly every weekend with his family trio, and most weekdays and some weekends with the other groups he'd formed. Known for his dedication to God and Gospel music, Everette gained the respect of his peers and community at an early age.

Everette as a teenager

After high school, Everette took a job in Johnson City, Tennessee, which eventually caused the family trio to disband. However, as one would expect, Everette was quick to form a quartet in his new location.

During this time he worked various jobs to support himself, but he lived for the opportunities to sing and perform. Work moved him from state to state, yet he always found time to play and sing Gospel music. The groups he played for shared the stage with some of the biggest names in Christian music, and after befriending these legends, he learned a great deal about both industry and ministry while on the road. These were lessons he would later teach his own children.

He was like a sponge, soaking up every drop of information or advice the full-time artists passed along. Everette took this information and worked at improving every aspect of his performance and ministry. Blessed with more than just great talent, Everette found that the Lord had also given him the opportunity to come to know many talented individuals who could offer expert advice: how to hold the microphone to get the maximum benefit; where to stand when someone is singing a solo; how to better communicate with the audience; how to determine what styles of songs mix well back-to-back. These were things Everette learned from the professional artists he looked up to.

These men and women offered more than just performance tips; they also gave practical advice, like how to save money while on the road, how to find the cheapest restaurants in town with the best food, and how to keep physically fit and healthy while traveling.

Southern Gospel music has always been an industry built on apprenticeship, and every artist can name several people who taught him or her "the ropes." Veteran performers traditionally pass along advice and tips to new singers and musicians who are making their way up the industry ladder, as Everette Greene was at that time.

Everette also learned from the crowds he played for. As the old saying goes, "Experience is the best teacher," and each road performance brought new and interesting situations to chalk up to experience. Mistakes can teach lessons better than anything, and any full-time performer can tell story after story of the mistakes he or she has made over the years.

The little child prodigy had come a long way from Baird's Creek, North Carolina, but his roots would not allow him to go too far.

Everette as a young man

Carolyn Townsend

CHAPTER TWO
I'M GOING ON WITH MY JESUS

"Music is harmony, harmony is perfection, perfection is our dream, and our dream is Heaven."

— Amiel

The family trio — Ralph, Tressie and Everette — was not the only family ministry traveling the local Christian circuit in that region of North Carolina in the '40s and '50s. One, in particular, had a couple of pretty daughters who were younger than Everette — the Townsend Family traveled in the same circle of revivals and singing conventions as the Greenes. Everette always looked forward to sharing the stage with them.

Clyde & Snow Townsend had four children, but only one of them performed in the family's singing group. The young soprano, Carolyn, caught Everette's eye right away, and eventually stole his heart. "I got her right out of the crib," Everette now likes to say, jokingly.

The young pianist eventually began playing accompaniment for the Townsend Family when Carolyn was just fourteen. The two never dated early on, but were always secretly fond of each other. "Oh, I loved to hear him play the piano," Carolyn recalls. "The sounds he created were just out of this world." And when it came to Carolyn, Everette couldn't decide which was most beautiful: her singing voice, her eyes, or her smile.

Even though she sang with her family, Carolyn had an intro- verted personality — always quiet and shy — whereas Everette was outspoken and outgoing. "He never met a stranger in his life," his mother says. "He could talk to any- body about anything!"

Carolyn (left) with her father, "Pop" Clyde Townsend, sister Donna (Cooke), and mother Snow Townsend

Opposites attract, and it seems that was what happened with Carolyn and Everette. After two years of singing and traveling together, they became good friends. However, anyone following their relationship in those days would never have guessed the two youngsters would end up tying the proverbial knot.

In 1961, Everette joined the Army and found himself ready to ship out for Fort Sill, Oklahoma. Just days before the twenty- three-year-old boarded a bus for Oklahoma, he asked Carolyn — just sixteen at the time — to marry him.

"He was getting ready to leave in a day or so, when out of the blue he asked me to marry him and go to Oklahoma," Carolyn vividly remembers. "I said 'yes,' and before I knew it, we were married and heading out for Oklahoma."

Although Everette had no fears when it came to performing in front of huge crowds, or when enlisting in the military to serve

Above is one of Everette's early Gospel groups, which included, left to right, Jim Stewart, Everette Greene, Wayne Shuford, Charles Burke and Mike Couper.

his country, he was more than a little anxious about asking Mr. Townsend for permission to marry his daughter. "I'll never forget when I asked him if I could marry her," Everette recalled. "He looked at Mrs. Townsend and said, 'Snow, where's my shotgun?'"

Everette and Carolyn married on March 13th, 1963 — without the aid of firearms. The young couple headed for

Everette, right, along with other Gospel group members in the 1960s.

Oklahoma while their parents sulked over not having their children so close at home. Everette and Carolyn missed their families as well, but they both worked at starting their own family and getting on with their lives.

While living in Lawton, Oklahoma, just as he had always done in the past, Everette found a local Gospel group and began playing piano — this time for the B.H. Goode Family. He managed his time as best he could so he would be able to play music without its interfering with his military job or family life. Everette was blessed with a wife that not only understood, but enjoyed it as well.

As Carolyn recalls, "For as long as we could remember, that's all we knew — and we enjoyed every minute of it!" Although Carolyn never performed with this group, she was on the road with them at every concert or revival. Her shy demeanor kept her

22

The Harmony Home Quartet, left to right, Snow Townsend, Clyde Tester, Carolyn and Everette Greene, and Clyde Townsend.

off the stage and out of the spotlight, but nothing would keep her from traveling with and supporting the man she loved.

Within a few months, they received the news that Carolyn was pregnant. The young couple was excited and immediately began making plans for the new arrival, but because Everette was working so much, he was unable to help his young bride keep up with everything during the pregnancy. So around three months before Everette's discharge, Carolyn traveled back to North Carolina so her family could assist her during the pregnancy.

After Everette's discharge from the Army, he worked several jobs, trying to earn enough money to support his growing family. However, he always found time to perform. More than just an expression of love for the piano and for entertaining, it was, Everette recognized, a call to minister for Christ through his music.

Most Southern Gospel music fans seem to think the artists and performers live a pampered life of luxury. Everette and Carolyn can testify that such is not a true depiction of their lives. They worked hard off stage simply to put food on the table. They tended gardens and raised chickens, hogs and other animals in order to get by.

Because Everette had played for so many groups and had helped form many of them, the success of the Greenes as we know them today was seemingly inevitable. Just as the veterans of his youth taught him, Everette took many singers and musicians under his wing.

For years young artists have sought the advice of Everette and Carolyn. Everette was never one to give fluff-filled answers. In fact, if you ask him a question, be sure you want the truth, because he won't lie to give you a glamorous picture. In fact, he is quick to tell you about the trials and stresses road life can bring. As he has told others, one must be sure he or she is called to this kind of life.

A certain quartet who was performing one night with the Greenes consisted of a group of kids just starting out. One of the young men approached Everette and said, "Mr. Greene, we'd like some advice — we're looking to buy a bus, and wonder what you think. We feel like it will help us, and we need the room and the storage." Everette said, "Well, you know buses are made by men, and they will tear up and break you. So, that's the first piece of advice: don't buy a bus!"

Maternal grandparents, Jesse and Lula James

"I advised them that if your heart is not in it, and God is not first, don't try to imitate it. It will break you up as a human; it will break you up as a family. And if you're not grounded in the Lord, or if you don't feel that He's got a calling on your life to do this, then stay out of it."

Everette was not trying to be harsh or come across with an attitude — he was just being honest; he knows what he is talking about. "I've been through it, and I've seen it," he explains. "I've experienced it. You can't really tell somebody exactly what they're getting into until they're in it. But I tried my best to warn them that it's not all peaches and cream — there are some hard times involved.

"I also told them that another good indication to watch for is when you make your record, and you have it on your product table, if the people in attendance for that performance don't go and buy your record, they've already told you how they feel about you.

"So, you better do things straight and honorable as you go, and one step at a time. You better wait until there is a desire for you out there in the marketplace. You better wait until the pastors start calling, wanting to book you in their churches, and promoters are calling wanting you to perform at their concerts. That's a good indication . . . and if you're not getting much radio air play, then forget it, because if the deejay doesn't see anything there, he's pretty smart — he pretty much knows which way you're going.

"It's one thing to sing for the Lord from your heart and feel like you have that calling; it's another thing just to do it for your own pleasure."

Through the years Everette and Carolyn have witnessed groups

Tim Greene was born on March 31st, 1964.

and families going through terrible financial difficulties because they end up singing to pay off a huge debt, instead of singing for God. As he put it, "All too often, I have seen many groups and families busted up because of the hardships financial difficulties bring, trying to pay for a bus and all the other expenses involved with traveling and singing professionally."

Everette also did much soul-searching in the early days, asking God if he had made the right choice to go full-time. "Sometimes back in those early days I'd question whether I had done the right thing; I'd keep going back and saying, 'Lord, I need some assurance.' That's the way it's always been with us; it's by faith, and faith alone."

Just a little past Everette and Carolyn's first anniversary, Tim Greene was born — on March 31st, 1964. The baby brought much happiness to his proud parents and to the entire extended family. But most new arrivals cause couples to slow their lives down and spend more time at home. This was not the case with the Greenes; Everette was playing and singing for groups just as much as before, if not more.

Baby Tim enjoyed traveling and listening to his father play the piano and sing. The future songwriter and musician "cut his teeth on" the music, you could say.

The Greenes moved to Florida for a few years, where Everette worked a couple of jobs and added a few more Gospel groups to his

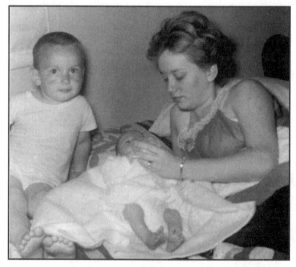

Tim, baby Kim and mom, Carolyn, in 1967

resume. But the hills of North Carolina kept calling for the young family to return, and they soon headed back to their hometown.

Tim was just three years old when the next family member entered the lives of the young Greene family. Little sister Kim Greene was born May 25, 1967, immediately giving the family the potential of becoming a quartet.

Everette eventually became successful in the lumber industry, but always found time for Gospel music. He bought into a lumber

Tim, Kim, Carolyn and Everette at Christmas 1967

company, and the growing family's future looked bright. Security is something every parent wants when raising children, and not having to worry about future financial problems made the hard times easier to bear.

Perhaps Kenneth R. Hendren said it best: "Security is our nearness to God, not our distance from danger." Everette and Carolyn did not put their trust in the lumber company; they put their trust in God. However, it was God that made the lumber company successful, and they knew it was God that kept putting food on their table.

When Kim was not quite seventeen months old, the youngest member of the Greene family made his debut. Tony Greene was born on October 17, 1968, and he would forever take his place as the beloved baby of the family.

Baby Kim, Ralph "Pop" Greene, Tim, and Great-Granny Greene

By this time, Tim was old enough to start attending grade school, and the bright little boy looked forward to the chance. He seemed to like it, as he did well in all subjects and was a well-behaved student. He was forever curious and enjoyed the classroom and various subjects.

A few years later Kim joined Tim on the school bus. Like Tim, she was a good student and loved being with other children. Being a good older brother, Tim kept a watchful eye on his little sister and always protected her.

Tim and Kim were both quiet and shy like their mother, Carolyn; Tony, as it turned out, showed strong signs as he grew that his personality was more like that of his father, Everette — outgoing, loving the spotlight and never considering anyone a stranger.

Tim holds little Tony while Kim holds her favorite baby-doll during the Christmas holiday season, 1968.

A young Tim Greene prepares to pass the football to Dad. Football continues to be Tim's favorite sport today.

When Tony joined his siblings in school a few years later, it seemed he was determined to let everyone know he was there: *move over everybody, Tony Greene has arrived*! Although he was considered the class clown, Tony did very well academically. Tony's personality garnered many friends; he knew how to lighten any mood. "You couldn't be around Tony ten minutes without laughing or being cheered up," Tim recalls.

In most ways, the Greenes children were no different from any other trio of siblings in the world. They had petty squabbles, called one another names, and made fun of each other's weaknesses. But at the same time, the children played well together and loved one another dearly. Like any other family, they could pick on one another, but if anyone else tried picking on any of them, the bully had all three to contend with.

Through the years, the children's interests changed with the passing fads and styles; their individual interests ranged from football, electric trains, and baseball, to dolls (Kim, of course), cars, trucks, wagons and motorcycles. But one thing was common to them all: their love of music.

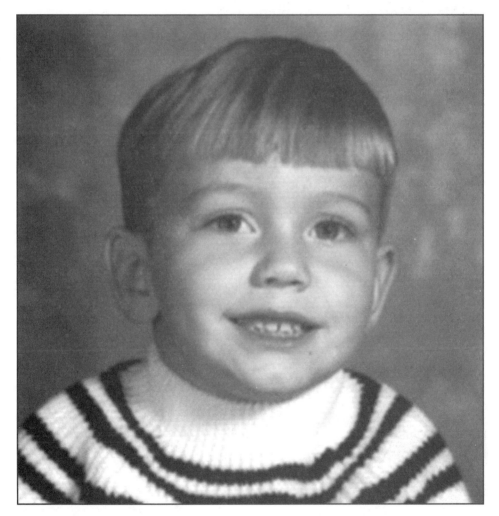

From the beginning, Tony Greene had an outgoing personality and was often called the "class clown."

Since they grew up around singers and musicians, it would seem apparent that the children had no choice but to succumb to the talents within them.

Some could argue that the children's talents came from Everette's side of the family; others, from Carolyn's side. However, the Greenes will be the first to tell you that any talent they all have came from God, and God alone.

"For as long as I can remember, Dad played the piano at the house," Tim remembers, grinning. "When I was six or seven, he began setting the three of us up on the piano bench and teaching us to sing 'Jesus Loves Me' and other songs. This went on every day for a couple of years; then I remember one day Kim falling into the harmony part without anyone teaching her. I don't remember exactly when that was, but I can remember the moment. I remember my dad was so excited because he knew she had a natural ear for the music."

No one would have ever guessed that these three little children would one day be at the top of the Southern Gospel charts, earning industry accolades and awards.

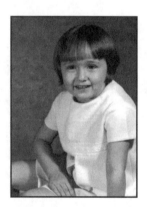

Tony	Kim	Tim

CHAPTER THREE
IT SURE SOUNDS LIKE ANGELS

"Music is well said to be the speech of
angels."

— Thomas Carlyle

It was while Everette was playing piano for the Pine Ridge Boys that his children began showing an interest in singing Gospel music. Tim was ten years old, Kim was seven and Tony was six when they communicated their desire to sing as a family group. Everette loved the idea and wanted them to sing, but he didn't want to push them into it. "I gave them a good out," he recalls, "because it can be confining, and you have to be married to it to have any success with it."

Back in those days competition was stiff, and Everette never dreamed the young family group would someday go full-time. "The Lord blessed in many ways," he explains, "and He showed us that this was the direction we needed to go."

The kids first started singing in their church youth choir in 1974. Carolyn remembers it well: "Kim would sit next to my mom to learn the alto part because she loved alto and didn't want to sing soprano. Tony — bless his heart — tried to sing and couldn't. He could not carry a tune and would cry for hours because of it. And Tim was a soprano, with a high-pitched voice."

When the kids first told their parents they wanted to sing, Everette gave it to them straight. "He said, 'Well, Tony, you can't sing,'" Carolyn remembers. "And Tony said, 'I can; I promise you I can sing.' And he would go to his bedroom and work on his singing constantly; within six months, sure enough, he was pretty strong."

Carolyn recalls Tim and Kim working on new areas, as well. "Tim could not sing anything but soprano," she remembers. "He worked hard to learn to sing tenor. We also needed a bass player,

A Happy Family: Everette and Carolyn, Kim, Tony and Tim

so he learned to play the bass guitar."

One Sunday afternoon the Pine Ridge Boys sang at a high school concert in Rutherfordton, North Carolina. The promoters of the sing asked Everette to bring the kids and let them sing a few numbers as well.

There were five to six hundred people in the audience that night, and it was the kids' first time singing anywhere publicly. Naturally the children were nervous, but their excitement overruled any apprehension.

"Kim, who's naturally shy, was barely seven at the time, and she was scared half to death," Carolyn remembered, with a chuckle. "The whole time they were on stage, she kept slowly pulling up at the sides of her dress. She must have thought, 'If I can't see the audience, then they won't be able to see me,' because by the time they finished, she had that dress over her head!"

The newly formed family group reminded Everette of his early years singing with his own mother and father. In fact, the young group began receiving calls from local pastors and promoters, booking them for small concerts and revivals at the same places he had played as a child.

Everette played the piano and sang bass, Tim played the bass guitar and sang the tenor part, Kim sang alto and Tony sang the high soprano part. However, changes later came when Tony's voice began changing. He moved to lead and baritone, and Kim moved to soprano.

Word quickly spread, and the young group of singers soon found themselves in high demand. They started accepting bookings, which led them into revivals and concerts in other counties and surrounding states.

"We piled everyone in our old Lincoln Continental and hit the road every weekend," Carolyn recalls. "We would put the sound equipment in the trunk and tie down the trunk-lid with a bungee chord, and the fumes would just about kill us. But we loved every minute of it; there were so many great memories made during that time."

"I remember the first little singing we did here in town," Tim said. "It was for a homecoming at Brushy Fork Baptist Church. We had never had any matching clothes before; I won't say we were dirt-poor, but most of our things were hand-me-downs. Somehow Mom had managed to go to Belk's Department Store and buy three V-neck sweaters that matched. So the three of us wore those sweaters, Kim with a skirt and Tony and I with slacks, and man, we thought we had made it big-time!"

Kim recalls: "Some of the most memorable times in the early years were the simplest things, like when Tim started writing songs, and we all wanted to help. In the winter, when we had snow days, the three of us would crawl up onto the boys' bunk beds and start writing songs. With guitar in hand, Tim would do most of the actual work, but he always made Tony and me feel as though we were important. We'd sit on those beds and sing those new songs and work out the harmony parts. Those are the precious memories that mean the most to me."

Even though the children were committed to Gospel music at an early age, they still had to take care of other things, too, like homework and school activities. It was always a balancing act as the children juggled schoolwork and responsibilities, along with their music practice and bookings.

In 1983 a series of events changed everything for the group. By this time Tim had a small studio in the basement of their house called Mountaintop Recording Studios and was learning the basics of the recording industry on an old eight-track recorder. One day someone brought by a song that captured his attention, and he shared it with the family. Written by Jeff Gibson of the trio *Heavenbound*, the song was "Gloryland."

"We recorded it and a few other songs one day," Tim recalls. "We didn't know if it was any good or not because we didn't have anything to judge it by. But Dad had a good friend in the industry named Charles Burke, who owned the *Singing Americans* at the time, and he sent him a copy of "Gloryland." Charlie told us we should send it out on a forty-five single and see what happens. We had no idea what that even meant, so we called him back and found out how to get a radio list and how to go about getting a single to the stations."

The young group had one hundred and fifty records produced in the forty-five rpm format, then sent them out to the biggest radio stations playing Southern Gospel music at the time.

"The response was unbelievable," Tim remembers. "Within six months it was on the *Singing News Magazine's* Top-Forty Chart. We couldn't believe it: we had a hit single!"

Southern Gospel music fans began calling their radio stations nationwide, asking about this new group called the Greenes, and wondering when they could see them in concert.

Although having a song on the charts was great, Everette and Carolyn wanted to make sure the kids kept everything in the proper perspective.

"We told them when we started that this was a ministry for the

Kim, Everette, Tim and Tony

Lord," Carolyn said. "When we got to where it was no longer a ministry, then we would go to the house. I'm proud that they have stayed true to the Lord and tried to honor Him and not make it a show or about the Greenes, but about God."

Their singing schedule began filling with more out-of-state concerts than regional bookings. Forced to turn down bookings too far to travel, the young group found themselves stretched far too thin because of the many not-too-distant concerts and revivals.

While Everette owned and managed the lumber company, Carolyn worked as a dispatcher for the Watauga County Sheriff's office, Tim worked at a local radio station, and together they farmed ten acres of cabbage. So the busy traveling schedule, combined with the already busy workweek, put pressure on everyone.

"It got to where we couldn't keep up," Carolyn remembers. "So, one weekend, on Friday, we agreed that we would ask the Lord what He wanted us to do because we couldn't continue the pace. We either had to quit the traveling and just sing locally, or get on with it.

"We battled with it all weekend, wondering what we were going to do. So Sunday night, before traveling back home, we decided to put it in God's hands. We said, 'All right, Lord, if you want us to go full-time and this is what you want for our lives, then send us a buyer for the lumber company.' That next morning at six a.m. a man called wanting to buy the lumber company — so we knew this was God's will."

"It blew my mind," Everette said. "I never would have dreamed of it happening so soon after the prayer, much less the very next day!"

"We knew God answered our prayers," Carolyn said with a laugh. "We had prayed hard, and we were convinced this is what the Lord wanted. So Everette sold the lumber company and I quit my job, and we went straight to the local Ford dealership and traded the old Lincoln for a van. We traveled in it for about six months before we realized the van just wasn't going to work out.

"So, in 1980, we went to Chattanooga, Tennessee, to buy our first bus. It was a thirty-five-foot MCI, and when we started home in it, we had to pull off at an exit and walk about a half-a-mile to McDonald's because Everette was afraid he wouldn't be able to turn it around!"

Everyone pitched in on transforming the bus into the home away from home for the Singing Greenes. "My dad did the interior for us," Carolyn remembers. "He built the bunks and did other work inside, and we traveled in it for a couple of years."

"Several months before he built the bunks, we just had mattresses lying in the floor," Tim recalls. "We had sheets tied up everywhere for privacy, so we could change clothes. A little each week, my grandfather worked on it until he ended up customizing it into a great looking bus for us."

No one thinks of the stress or hardships brought on by road ministry, but anyone who has traveled full-time will tell you there are more lean years than those with your head above the water. The Greenes survived many setbacks, financial problems and physically and mentally draining road fatigue.

"Everette was about ready to call it quits every Monday," Carolyn recalls with a chuckle. "It was hard trying to stay on the road. We had many lean times, for sure. We would write checks on Thursday and put them in the mail and hope and pray that we could make them good by the time we got home on Monday. The kids were in school, so making sure they kept their grades up was tough enough, but having to take them out of school for certain concerts and events was really difficult."

"When you say 'lean,' they were *very* lean," Everette agreed. "It was all by faith. We did not know from one week to the next if we were going to get a payday or not, and the payday was usually spent before we got it."

Stress and hardship cause questions to arise, even from a believer with extraordinary faith. "I questioned the Lord many times," Everette confessed. "I'd pray, 'Lord, are You sure this is what You want? If it is, we need Your help.' But He always made a way — not always on our time, but He always came through, in *His* time."

"But we were a family," Carolyn added, "and it wasn't as hard for us, I guess. Because the kids were so young, it wasn't as hard for us as it would have been had they been grown, and we would've had to make salaries for everybody. It was hard — don't get me wrong — but it was also so fulfilling to go out and see the glory of the Lord and His presence. The material things didn't really matter."

Through the hard times and the good times, the Greenes stood firm in what God blessed them to do. Instead of causing dissension, as it has with some other groups, the lean times only pulled the Singing Greenes closer.

"We've always been a close family," Carolyn said. "But when you're working for the Lord and everyone has one common goal, it just makes everything a lot easier."

Carolyn and Everette always told the kids to mind God and never feel as though they were forced to travel and sing for a living. They wanted their children to know that following God's will was more important than anything else in their lives.

"That's something we wanted to make clear from the start," Carolyn said. "We told the kids when they were growing up, 'This may be what you want to do right now, but when you're grown, you may want to do something else.' So, we encouraged them to have something to fall back on in case they did not want to continue to do this."

So Kim, accordingly, went to school to become a hairdresser — and keeps her license up to this day. Tony has worked in the funeral business since he was a teenager, and Tim has the recording studio and could always go back into radio.

"We never wanted them to feel like they were stuck doing this," Carolyn said. "We tried to encourage them, and let them know that if this is what they wanted, then we would back them and support them and do everything we could to help them, but they didn't have to do this. But they kept pushing us because they knew it was what God wanted in their lives. We could say today, 'Boys, it's over,' and they would find a way to go on. And Kim's always loved it as well, if not better, than her brothers."

The group released its next single to radio, called "It Sure Sounds Like Angels." "I think that song really helped us get known," Tim asserts. "We asked well-known pianist and producer Eddie Crook to help us with it. We recorded it, but we asked Eddie to help us get it distributed better, and it was a big success. A larger number of radio stations got to hear what we were trying to do because of it.

"A woman from our home church, Jean Canter, wrote that song. Whether good or bad, our harmony was so different from what everybody else was doing, that I think that was what helped our music stand out. And only God could have done that because, as far as we were concerned, we were just singing! We didn't have a plan; we just thought if we were singing about angels, we should try to sound like angels."

Everyone in the group has always had a job to do, some more than others. Although she has a beautiful voice herself, Carolyn has chosen to work behind the scenes, taking care of the laundry on the road, seeing to their meals, and managing the product table. Tony serves as the emcee, and he and Tim handle the bookings and setting up the equipment before the concerts. In those early days, Kim handled all the song arrangements, and Everette drove the bus. He would often drive all night, and then perform with the children at each concert or church.

"It got to where he couldn't drive all night and sing, too," Carolyn remembers. "So he told the kids to go on as a trio and let him just drive the bus, and then rest."

When Everette stopped performing, the children wondered if they would be able to go on without him. But Everette cheered them on from the sidelines, then slipped into the bus to get some sleep before having to start driving to the next state or town.

"Our first number one song was 'When I Knelt the Blood Fell,' which Tim wrote," Carolyn recalls. "I'll never forget: we were in West Virginia when we got word that it had gone number one."

It would be the first of five number one songs the Greenes have had as of this writing.

One of the biggest moments for the young trio came when they first performed at the National Quartet Convention in 1983.

"Kim had spent hours and hours looking for the perfect dress

for the convention," Carolyn recalls. "At that time it was in Nashville, and you had to go up steps to get on stage. Tim led the others up the steps, Kim was second, and Tony followed close behind. In fact, Tony followed a little *too* close behind, because he stepped on Kim's new dress and ripped the hemline, in full view of the crowd. Still they went straight up on cue and began singing, as poor Kim stood there in front of the crowd at the National Quartet Convention with tears running down her face — because Tony had torn her beautiful new dress."

Tony recalls that incident well, relating it in his typical humorous style: "Here the crowd was just loving it, thinking Kim was really singing 'in the Spirit,' because those big tears were just flowing down her cheeks — when really she was just upset that her brother had torn her favorite dress!"

Through the years, the Greenes have had full support from their home church in Boone, North Carolina. Westview Baptist has served as home for the Greene and Townsend families for decades.

"They formed that church when I was about twelve years old," Carolyn recalls. "We took each of our children to the altar when they were born and dedicated them to God. We prayed, 'Lord they're not ours — You've only loaned them to us. You take them and make them what You want them to be. Use them in a way that You see best,' and I feel that is precisely what He has done."

Westview Baptist Church

The Greenes have found more than spiritual blessings from Westview Baptist; the church has also supported them financially as a type of missionary ministry during the lean years.

"We couldn't have made it through some of the hard times had God not used Westview

Baptist to support the Greenes," Carolyn remembers with obvious gratitude. "Because of their love and support, we were able to keep doing what He called us to do."

This is the same church that Tim has pastored since 1993; Tony serves as the minister of music. To this day the Greenes attempt to schedule their appointments so they are able to be in their home church every Sunday for worship.

Westview Baptist Church is located on the 105 Bypass in Boone, North Carolina, just across from the Coca-Cola distribution center. If you are visiting the area, you would be heartily welcomed to worship with this wonderful congregation. Tim preaches on Sundays at 11 a.m. and Wednesday night for prayer service at 7 p.m., and Sunday School begins at 10 a.m. on Sunday morning.

Tony Greene polishes the Greenes bus

Westview also has special services throughout the year including special singing with the best in Southern Gospel music. The Florida Boys, The Comptons, The Dixie Melody Boys, Barbara Fairchild and of course, the home group, The Greenes, sing often at Westview. They also have some excellent visiting preachers like Phil Hoskins, Zeno Groce, Larry Walker, Gary Frazier, and many others.

The Greenes have many friends to thank for their endless support and love over the years, and Westview Baptist is at the top of the list. Of course, there were many pastors, promoters and industry people who have helped as well, and the family has never forgotten any of them.

***

"Splendor and glory my eyes shall see, when I see Jesus who died for me; Heaven will be prettier than I've ever dreamed; Christ's splendor and glory I'll see."

— By Tim Greene, "Splendor," *Choral Favorites, Southern Gospel Style*

The Greenes — Kim, Tony and Tim — perform at the Annual Gospel Singing Jubilee at High Country Fairgrounds, at Boone, NC.

The Greenes

Catch the excitement in ministry

CHAPTER FOUR
JESUS' ROCKING CHAIR

"Instead of weeping when a tragedy
occurs in a songbird's life, it sings
away its grief. I believe we could well
follow the pattern of our feathered
friends."

— Robert S. Walker

The Greenes knew that having sold-out concerts and good record sales depended on radio airplay. They also knew that to get good radio airplay, they must first record great songs. Finding a potential hit is harder than most folks realize; for one reason, there are far more professional recording artists than professional songwriters. Because of this, the best songs are not on the market long.

Could this be the reason Tim Greene first became a songwriter? Was it because the group needed fresh material? No. Tim became a songwriter for many of the same reasons he became a singer and musician. God blessed him with the talent and the desire, and he finds songwriting to be a means of expressing His relationship with Christ and helping others vocalize what is in their hearts. A songwriter gives singers and listeners the words to praise God with.

Tim grew up listening to Southern Gospel music and at an early age knew most of the great songwriters by name. He paid

Tim

close attention to how the veteran writers composed their songs and began experimenting with words and chords himself. Before long, he was writing songs and performing them in concerts. When he witnessed lives being changed because of his songs, he knew this was no game. Seeing men, women, boys and girls of all ages give their hearts to Christ because of a song he wrote was a good indication that God's hand was in the song's creation. Tim seemed compelled to compose extremely personal lyrics that were biblically sound.

"Our first goal was always — as it still is today — to focus on what God wants us to do," Tim said. "When we are picking songs for an album, or picking songs to sing in Birmingham, Alabama, or wherever we may be, the first thought is, 'What will be most effective in bringing the audience into a worship experience? What will lead people to know Christ on a more personal level?' because that's the reason we do what we do."

Tim has penned five number one songs and countless top 80 hits. He won the 1998 Dove Award for Southern Gospel Song of the Year, yet his motivation for songwriting is getting to see his songs help lead people to know Jesus Christ as their personal Savior.

Being the eldest of the three children, Tim saw the road experiences a little differently than his siblings.

"When I think back on those early years, I can't help but laugh," Tim recalls. "While Kim was into Barbie dolls and Tony was interested mostly in cartoons, I was just getting interested in girls. I was a young teenager, and just like any other boy that age, I went through many awkward stages. But my dating experience in high school, most of the time, was asking a young lady to ride with my family as we traveled somewhere to sing. That was the only thing we could do, so most of my dates were singing dates!"

"They were teenagers, and we wanted them to act like teenagers," Carolyn said. "We were proud of them and wanted them to enjoy life. We wanted them to be as average as they possibly could be."

The FCC granted Tim a radio operator's license when he was

Tim as a teen

just fourteen, and he began working as a deejay for radio station WATA 1450 on the A.M. dial. He worked there off and on for roughly six years until it became too difficult to balance the radio work with his road schedule.

Fortunately, this radio experience helped Tim understand what radio stations were looking for when picking new songs. It also gave him valuable knowledge of listeners' tastes, thanks to their feedback concerning song styles and lyrics.

So how does a shy, quiet kid from "Smalltown, USA," become a popular radio disc jockey? In school, Tim had hardly spoken at all, yet suddenly he found himself broadcasting to thousands of people. Like many in the radio industry, Tim felt comfortable speaking into a microphone where listeners could not see him. He fell in love with the medium and probably would have made a career out of it, had the singing career not taken off when it did.

Tim's love for radio is just as strong today as it was the first time he spoke over a microphone. He currently hosts a syndicated radio show called *America's Gospel Countdown*, which airs on over 160 stations weekly.

Another love in Tim's life is football. Anyone who knows him can tell you he is a big fan of the NFL's Carolina Panthers. The telephone that sits at the controls of his recording studio is in the shape of a full-sized football helmet with the Carolina Panthers logo on it.

Tim played football through his eighth-grade year; he wanted to play more, but his schedule would not allow it. It's not that he feels he has missed anything in life — he simply enjoyed playing the game.

Radio wasn't the only job he held in his younger days. Tim also worked part-time at a business called Auto Shine, washing and waxing automobiles. The job helped him earn some extra spending money, while giving him a sincere respect for the men and women who work in that field.

The extra money always came in handy when he was dating steady, which wasn't often, again because of his hectic road schedule.

Then, one day in a little town called Rowlett, Texas, the "singing dates," as Tim called them, would end.

Concert promoter Lamond Vernor and his family were close friends with Kirk Talley and had invited the Talley Trio to their home for dinner one evening while the group was in town for a concert.

Mr. Vernor had a daughter named Amy, who worked as a lifeguard at a local water-park. During dinner, Kirk asked Amy if she would mind escorting Roger, Debra and him to the water-park the following day for some rest and relaxation. Amy agreed and made plans for the outing.

The next morning, Amy rushed off to the hotel parking lot to meet the Talleys. However, when she arrived, she didn't find Roger, Debra and Kirk waiting for her; instead, she found Kirk and a bunch of guys she did not know. Roger and Debra wanted to sleep in, so Kirk invited Tim and Tony Greene, with their drummer, Robbie Stevens, to join them. The Greenes were staying in the same hotel and the young men were getting restless.

"I was so humiliated," Amy remembers. "I'd just crawled out of bed and threw on some clothes without fixing my hair or putting on makeup. So I felt like crawling under a bench or something."

Amy

The only words spoken between them were those of Tim asking Amy if he could borrow her towel because he had dropped an ice-cream cone on his shoes.

It must have been an impressive towel, because Tim went back to the hotel and told his mother he had just met the woman he was going to marry.

"I didn't have to talk with her," Tim remembers. "All my life I had always known the woman God had for me would have olive-colored skin with dark eyes and dark hair. But I had no idea that she would live a thousand miles away from me. Especially since we hardly ever sang in Texas, and I sure wasn't out there looking for a wife."

Kirk invited Amy to come to the concert the next night and listen to the Greenes perform.

"Judging by Tony's accent, I didn't really want to go listen to this bunch of hillbillies," Amy remembers with a chuckle. "But they wouldn't stop bugging me until I agreed to go."

"You've heard how Tony talks today," Tim interjected; "well, he was a hundred times worse, back then."

"I thought Tim told me the concert was in Aubrey, which is an hour and a half from where I lived," Amy continued, "but he said *Alney*, Texas, which was four hours away, so when I didn't show, he thought I had just stood him up."

"Come to find out, she just went to the wrong place," Tim explained with a grin.

"It made him so mad, thinking I had stood him up, that he called that Monday to ask why I didn't show. Then it got to where we would talk nearly every day on the phone and before long, we became good friends."

Tim and Amy soon started a long-distance courtship, mostly by mail and telephone, but occasionally they would get to see each other in person.

"For the first year and a half, her dad wouldn't even let me hold her hand," Tim said. "And he wouldn't let me talk to her that much, but he eventually warmed up."

"But the positive thing we had going for us was that my dad was the biggest Southern Gospel fan in the world," Amy said.

"Oh, he still is," Tim agreed. "We would never have met had it not been for her dad. He was good friends with the Talleys and booked them in some churches when they first started, and then as our relationship grew stronger, he started booking us some, too."

"To give you an idea how big of a Southern Gospel fan my dad is, for my seventeenth birthday, he gave me tickets to the National Quartet Convention!" Amy recalled with a laugh. "The whole family went to the Quartet Convention, and that was the official first date for Tim and I. That was when the lovebug really bit me, and I never turned back."

The couple began building a strong relationship over the telephone.

"I fell in love with Tim from the inside out," Amy said. "Most relationships start from the outside with a physical attraction."

"We lived so far apart," said Tim, "so we fell in love over the phone. I fell in love with her voice and what she had to say. I guess we did it backwards from everyone else, but we fell in love with each other's minds, dreams and thoughts. I just think the Lord had the perfect woman set aside for me, and let me see that she was the one for me.

"I have heard Gospel singers mention how they could sing every night but their wives gave them such a hard time over being gone so much. I have heard others say that singing and traveling creates many problems with their wives. But I can honestly say that we have been married since 1986 and I have never once heard Amy complain about me going. She has always encouraged me to go for Jesus, and as long as I knew in my heart

Tony, Amy and Tim

that that's what I'm supposed to do, she's been supportive."

Amy has made many behind-the-scenes contributions to the singing group over the years, and the whole family knows how important she is to the family and group.

"Her best quality is her people skills," Tim said. "And this is something that she has helped me with so much. My heart has always been in writing music, preaching and singing on the road. But God gave her the gift of making others feel welcomed, special and loved. She has taught me to treat everyone with the highest of respect, and to take the time to shake their hands and tell them they are looking good.

"I remember the first thing she told me after hearing us sing for the first time. She said, 'You're not smiling enough!' She has helped me with things like that for as long as I've known her. They say the woman makes the man, and I can honestly say that she makes me a better man; she makes me a better Tim, and she really is the glue of the family."

> More beautiful than rubies,
> More precious than pearls;
> She is to me more lovely —
> This woman that I love.
>
> — Tim Greene, "More Beautiful Than
> Rubies," from *At the Cross*

Not only were Tim and Amy married in 1986, but he accepted the call to preach that same year. He began booking for revivals, camp meetings, concerts and other special services — many of them booking the Greenes to sing and Tim to preach in the same services. But some churches wanted to book Tim alone, preaching and singing solo.

Wanting to be a better minister, Tim decided to become educated in the sacred field. He studied for three years at Trinity

Kim and the lovely bride on Amy's wedding day

Bible School in Newbergh, Indiana, then earned his doctorate from New Wine Theological Institute in Dallas, Texas. However, Doctor Tim Greene never uses the title while preaching or ministering; he wanted the education, not the title or prestige.

In 1992 he became the pastor of his home church, Westview Baptist — the same church where his grandfather, Clyde Townsend, was head of the Deacon Board from 1960 to 1986.

"Westview is a small church of about two hundred people who have only one goal: to lift up Jesus as Savior of the world," Tim said. "They are just a great bunch of folks who love the Lord."

Devotions are broadcast from the church each weekday morning at 8 a.m. on 100.7 FM WZJS. Anyone wishing to read about the church and its members on the Internet can do so by visiting http://www.peopleofwestview.org.

Daughter Brittany came into Tim and Amy's lives in 1990, and has brought more sunshine than the couple would have ever imagined.

Tim, Amy and Brittany

"Brittany is really the superglue of our family," Amy said as she explained the role she has played in their family.

"Brittany is a child that has never been a child," Tim said with a laugh. "I think Brittany has really helped Amy and me grow up more than we have helped her grow up."

"She reminds me so much of my mother," Amy said, smiling.

Amy's mom, who was referred to as "Mimi," passed away in 1997. When Brittany was younger, one of Mimi's biggest thrills was to make sure Brittany was perfectly dressed and groomed. Tim explained, "I mean, Brittany didn't go to McDonald's with

Brittany Greene

her unless she had every strand of hair in perfect place and ribbons everywhere."

"Brittany has always been the parent to Tim and me," Amy said and nodded, agreeing with Tim. "She has always been a good child."

In the video *In His Eyes*, Tim talked about his unique relationship with Brittany and discussed the challenges of being a father while also being on the road in full-time ministry.

"From the time Brittany was about ten years old, she would call me every night when I was on the road — maybe around 10:00 or 10:30 — and we would say our evening prayers together," Tim said.

"Nightly I would remind her that everything was going to be all right, and that there were angels watching over her at her bedside."

Tim later wrote a song that expressed his love for Brittany and their special moments in prayer.

Angels Around Your Bed

Oh, tonight I'm so far away from you,
How I wish I could suddenly be there.
To tell you I love you,
Like a hundred times before,
To hold you and to stroke your hair.

But I'm in another time zone altogether,
And sleep is not easily found;
A split-second prayer escapes into the air
And I pray as you lay your body down

There'd be angels around your bed, Little
Darlin',
Angels around your bed —
Safe from harm at the dying of the day
With angels around your bed.

— By Tim Greene, "Angels Around Your Bed,"
from *In His Eyes*

"I'll never forget when we found out Amy was carrying Brittany," Tim said. "I woke up in the middle of the night and began shaking Amy, saying, 'Hey, wake up, wake up, wake up!' Amy mumbled, 'What's going on? What's wrong?' and I said, 'The Lord just showed me that we were going to have a baby!' and she said, 'No, you're just having a dream; go back to sleep!' — but a month later we found out she was pregnant during that time."

"He did the same thing the second time I was pregnant," Amy said. "It was not even time for me to show any signs or anything, but I convinced the doctor to give me a blood test. The doctor didn't want to give me a test but I said, 'You don't understand — we've been through this before!'"

"God not only told me we were going to have another child, but He also told me it would be a boy, and his name would be

John," Tim recalled. "And it wasn't long before we went through a miscarriage and lost the baby."

"John — the forerunner of Christ," Amy whispered with a smile.

"That was one thing that really helped us during that time," Tim explained. "When I told my grandmother I didn't understand why God would take this baby after telling me his name would be John, she said, 'Well, what was John? He was the forerunner of greater things to come."

This was a traumatic event in the young couple's lives, and the only refuge Tim could find was in family, prayer and songwriting.

Allison Stinson was a fan of the Greenes from many years back and attended many of the Greenes concerts. When she was 16 years old, Allison was diagnosed with chronic juvenile rheumatoid arthritis (CJRA), yet was able to attend The Greenes' Homecoming in 1993 on crutches.

The first night of Homecoming Tim announced that he and Amy were expecting their second child. However, later that week, he had the painfully difficult task of explaining to the crowd that his wife Amy was unable to attend because she had suffered a miscarriage.

Allison, who was

Tim and Amy Greene

in the audience that night and was overwhelmed with sympathy for the young couple, felt the urge to do something to help comfort them.

A month later, Allison was hospitalized with the second most severe case of CJRA the hospital had ever seen, and began chemotherapy treatments.

Allison was kept home from school because she became so sick from the treatments that she nearly died. She got out of the hospital just in time to see The Greenes as they were passing through her hometown. During that concert, Tim, once again, shared the pain he and Amy suffered during their miscarriage. Allison felt such a burden for them and knew that God was prompting her to help, but she was not sure how she could.

The next night, she went into her room and began praying for God to comfort her and give her peace with her health until things got better. She also began to pray for Tim and Amy. She picked up a pen and, without even thinking, wrote the words to a poem. After reading over the words, she first thought it was silly.

"I thought that Tim would laugh at me," Allison remembers. "I was terrified to give the poem to him, but something kept tugging at my heart."

Two months later, Allison gave the poem to Amy Lambert for her opinion. Amy prompted her to give the poem to Tim.

"He was touched by the poem and appreciated the gesture," Allison recalls, "and I thought that was the end, but a couple of months later I learned that Tim had written a song from a line in the poem. That was such an honor."

The song was "Jesus' Rocking Chair". The Greenes recorded it and the song went straight to number one in April of 1995, and captured Song of the Year at the 1995 Diamond Awards.

Jesus' Rocking Chair
By Allison Stinson

Daddy I'm watching down on you
And I just heard you say

That you and Mommy lost a baby
How sad you were that day

I want you to know I love you
And I appreciate the thought

But if you could see me now so happy
And I'm so much better off

I know you and Mommy would care for me
And I'd be surrounded by love

But just remember I'm watching you
And I'm waiting for you above

I know you and Mommy wanted me
And so did my family

But Jesus had a pair of baby wings
And He needed me worse you see

For if I'd come to the world
And taken the Greene name

I might have only been a failure
And brought you only shame

But don't worry about me now
I'm safe and secure in His care

And just in case Mommy worries
Tell her Jesus has a rocking chair

So keep singing and preaching for Jesus
And soon you'll come to see me

The first thing I want you to do
Is sing a song for me

Tell Mommy I love her too
And I can't wait for her to hold me

I'll be waiting by the river
There's no way she could miss me

Tell my big Sissy Brittany
I can't wait for her to play with me

And until we all meet up here
Give her the love you had for me

© 1995 Allison Stinson

"In a short time we have suffered much loss and a lot of pain," Tim said, "but at the same time, I believe God has made us a stronger family because of everything. Our son, John, is still our precious child who happens to be in Heaven with Jesus."

During a solo concert in the late-1990s, Tim confessed to an audience that he occasionally wonders what John would have been, had he been born. Amy and Tim have speculated if John would have eventually been a doctor, lawyer, or possibly another member of the family's music ministry. Regardless of the pain of loss that still lingers, Tim said that they are completely satisfied to know that their baby is in the arms of Jesus. "That's reassuring for us to know that someday we will see him, and that he is loved and happy in Heaven with our Lord Jesus."

Hold on, Tony!

CHAPTER FIVE
I'M SO HAPPY

"A merry heart doeth good like a
medicine."

— Proverbs 17:22

"The first time I met the Greenes, I was about sixteen years old," *Singing News* managing editor Danny Jones recollected. "I was living with my parents in Georgia at the time, and we attended every Southern Gospel concert that came to town. One day we bought tickets to see a new group called The Singing Greenes.

"Kim was eighteen and Tim was about twenty — they were just a bunch of kids. As I stood in the parking lot, I remember Tony Greene getting off the bus, and my first impression was: this guy is a loudmouthed, obnoxious, spoiled brat. My feelings haven't particularly changed," Danny added as he chuckled.

Always a ham for the spotlight, Tony Greene was a natural when it came to communicating with crowds. He has been the Greenes' emcee from the beginning and always knew how to make people laugh. It's rather obvious he loves to talk, and he loves the people he talks to.

"The Lord has definitely given Tony the gift of gab," Tim Greene said with a snicker. "In fact, Tony can connect with people in a way that Kim or I can't. Whether it's telling funny stories, jokes or just having a regular conversation, he has a gift for making people feel comfortable. He's incredible; I have never seen anyone that he would not be willing to talk with or speak to.

"We were in an airport not long ago and sat down to get our shoes shined while waiting on a flight, and every person who sat down near us, Tony would speak to them. He'd say, 'Hey, buddy, how ya doin'?' Well after a few minutes of this, someone from behind us said, 'What's that guy running for?' He thought Tony was a politician or something!"

Tony is someone who not only has the gift of gab, but his quick wit can easily turn any situation into a laugh.

"With Tony, there was never a dull moment on the road," Kim remembers. "And if you ever bobbled anything up in front of an audience, you knew he was going to take it and run with it. I'll never forget one Sunday morning when I was around thirteen or fourteen, I had one of the most embarrassing moments of my life. I'd just started  wearing high-heeled shoes, and while walking down the steps of the platform, my heel caught a snag in the carpeting. Trying to keep my balance, I fell face-forward and slid under the front pew. Out of the blue, Tony jumps down in front like a baseball umpire and yells, 'Safe!' Needless to say, the congregation fell apart."

Tony was not always so quick-witted; there were a few memorable occasions where his tongue worked a tad faster than his brain. Fortunately, most of those occasions were when he was younger.

"Oh, I'll never forget when he was around ten years old and we were in Logan, West Virginia," Carolyn said with a smile. "We were singing at an outside concert and the promoter had made room down close to the stage for several severely handicapped people. Some of them were in wheelchairs and a few were on cots. So Tony, of course, was only trying to be polite and make them feel welcome. He meant to say, 'I would like to dedicate this next song to the invalids here in front of the stage.' But what stumbled out of his mouth was, 'I would like to dedicate this next song to these *infidels* in front of the stage!'"

Afterwards, of course, Tony found out from embarrassed family members that an "infidel" is someone who doesn't have any religious beliefs — not someone who is sick or handicapped (an "invalid").

Perhaps one of the best stories about Tony Greene was published in the *Singing News Magazine*, told by Danny Jones. The name of the article, entitled "Lifestyles of the Not So Rich and Famous," told the story of the time Danny tagged along with the Greenes on a weekend trip. Here is the story in its entirety, courtesy of Danny and the *Singing News Magazine*:

Here at *Singing News*, there's tremendous activity on our Internet mailing lists. Intense discussions on various aspects of our music take place between industry members and fans on a daily basis. But there are some milder moments, too. About a year ago, I posted an account of a horrendous trip I had just completed. Little did I know that was the start of something I have to do periodically. I never dreamed anyone would be interested in road life, but there's a certain segment of people out there who crave that kind of story. I get quite a bit of e-mail from these people, wanting more. However, no story has generated the mail this Columbus, Ohio, story did. In fact, there's hardly a night that goes by that someone doesn't come up to the

SINGING NEWS table and say, "Hey, you're the one that..."

Naturally, there are a lot of people who overhear this comment and I have to tell the whole story to those who don't have access to e-mail.

So, for those of you that have called, here is what happened one chilly October 1996 evening in Columbus, Ohio. Before I begin, let me just say one thing: IT WAS TONY GREENE'S FAULT. Tony promotes several concerts around the country each year. One of those is an annual October sing in Columbus and in 1996, the date fell during a weekend Tony had chosen not to book any other engagements. Thus, he called my office and invited me to travel with them.

Everything went fine traveling to Columbus and with that evening's concert. After loading up and departing the auditorium, we did what every group does following a concert — look for a place to eat. We headed along the interstate and pulled into the first reputable restaurant we saw. We got off the bus and went into the restaurant. However, we discovered there would be an hour's wait. Not wanting to wait that long, we climbed back aboard the bus and headed off in search of another restaurant.

This scenario repeated itself about three times. Finally, we pulled into the parking lot of another restaurant and Tony, Tim and their dad, Everette, head into it to eat. By this time, I've decided I could do with a light snack, so instead of going into the restaurant with them, I'll just visit the little convenience store that's next door.

Carolyn (Mom) Greene and Milena Parks are still on the bus as I start to get off of it so I call back to them, "I'm getting off the bus — don't let them leave without me." "Okay" comes the response. Here's where things go awry. Even though Carolyn and Milena were still on the bus, they were in two different rooms on the bus at the time I left. I didn't know that! They were discussing something and were having to use their voices loudly to hear each other in their respective rooms. You've probably picked up that the "Okay" I heard was one of the ladies' response to a comment the other had made.

So here I go, be-bopping off the bus and into the store. I'm in there all of three minutes, pick up my snacks, pay for them, walk out and head around the corner to where the bus is. Or was. Sure enough, the Greenes have left yet another restaurant. My first thought is that Tony has just moved the bus to make leaving the lot a little easier. Nope.

So there I was: standing with my drink and chips in a parking lot in Columbus, Ohio, that looked a lot like those sights you see on programs like *Unsolved Mysteries* or *Cops*. Even though I'm not overly concerned with my predicament (thank goodness I had my wallet with me, so I could have rented a car to get home), the drug deal (that's what it seemed to be) going down across the street gave me serious doubts about wanting to hang around to see if the Greenes realized I was not on the bus.

Right after we had left the auditorium, Tony remarked he needed to get fuel before they left town. So, remembering this, I decide to give the Ohio State Patrol a call to see if they can catch the bus at a nearby truck stop I guessed Tony would stop at. I walk over to a phone booth and not finding a directory to use get a non-emergency number, I call 911.

Before I go on, let me pause to remind you that Columbus, Ohio, is a big college football town. Columbus places college football on a pedestal just behind God. And this particular Saturday night, the home team had played their biggest rival. And won.

You can imagine the celebrations that were going on. When you get a city that size, filled with crazed football fans who are celebrating with various quantities of liquid refreshments, police officers get lots of overtime.

I make my call and when an officer answers, I explain my situation. There's nothing but silence on his end. Then he asks me to hold. When he gets back on the line, I can barely hear him because of all the laughing that's going on in the background. His exact words were, "Sir, forgive us for laughing. We've been chasing drunks and breaking up fights all night and this is a welcomed relief! We don't mean to laugh, but we're glad you called!" I'm standing outside in the cold, three hundred miles from home and no way to get there, an unwilling witness to possible criminal activity, and they're glad I called! What a ministry!

To make a long story short, I had to explain the situation to what seemed to be five or six different patrolmen. I just hope that stupid 9-1-1 tape doesn't show up on *Rescue 9-1-1* someday. Meanwhile on the Greenes' bus, Tony is still heading East, about 10 minutes from the truck stop. Carolyn comes up to the driver's area and they start talking. Tony asks his mom to go to his room and get his jacket (to use when he fuels the bus). She opens the door to his room and ... "WEEEEEEE LLLLLEEEEFFFFFTTTTT DAAAAANNNY!"

I found out later that Tony had thought I turned in for the night (I was using the spare bunk in Tony's room) while we were parked at the restaurant. Anyway, he goes on to the truck stop, fuels and heads back to the restaurant. (At least he was in a hurry, right?)

Back at the phone booth, I'm still on the phone with the state patrol, "ministering" to them. I can safely say, though, one of the prettiest sights I've seen in my 16+ years of Southern Gospel Music is that of the Greenes' bus topping the hill, coming toward the phone booth. Tony pulls up, opens the door, looks at me and says, "I guess I can forget about a cover, huh?"

***

"Tony is probably one of the hardest working concert promoters I have ever seen," Danny said. "He will bust his rear-end to make sure a concert goes off well. The one thing I can say about him is that never in my life have I known of him to cut a group's pay or tell them 'I'll make it up to you next week' or something like that. He's always done exactly what he said he was going to do. As far as his commitments to the groups, he always honors them. I guess he's had that happen to him, and he knows what it's like, and he won't do it to anyone else."

Tony knows the industry and knows the people. He is a smart business

Tony catches up on his reading

leader and has always been successful, whether promoting concerts or handling any other business he has ventured into. But even though there are important business aspects in music min-

istry that must be attended to, Tony is also quick to point out that it is Christ's ministry first and foremost. "It's about surrendering to Jesus, and ministering to His children. We must stay out of the way and allow the Spirit to flow through us. The business side of the ministry comes after all that, so that we are simply faithful stewards of the resources the Lord gives us."

"Another thing about Tony I've noticed," Danny adds, "is that he is a smart promoter. He may not always hire the groups that he would like to hear himself, but he knows what will put people in the seats, and that is who he brings in to sing."

Tony has worked with some of the biggest promoters in the music industry, either as an artist or as a partner in the promotions.

"The first time I remember ever talking with Tony, he called me on the telephone," industry-leading promoter, Ray Flynn remembers. "And every time he would say anything, it was 'buddy' this and 'buddy' that, and I thought, 'I don't even know this guy, and he's calling me 'buddy' every other sentence. He kept asking me why I thought so many of my concerts were successful, and things like that. Well, I thought he was just pumping me for information.

"Eventually, the Greenes had something that came out that I liked, and I thought that they would work well at a concert we were going to do, and so, I finally booked them. A few days before the concert, Tony called me and asked how the concert was looking. I told him it was sold out, and he said, 'Well, you know why it's sold out, don't you?' and I said, 'Why is that?' and he said, 'Because you've got the Greenes on it!' Forget the fact the last ten or twelve concerts I had promoted were all sell-outs; it was all because of the Greenes! Maybe it did have something to do with the Greenes — I don't know."

Tony and Ray would eventually work many concerts together; the pair later partnered with a few others to form Abraham Promotions, a company that promotes concerts and annual events such as *Singing in the Sun* in Myrtle Beach.

"Tony brings a unique perspective to concert promoting," Ray said. "He is able to give the perspective of a promoter, as well as the perspective of an artist. He understands how critical it is to keep the costs down for more fans to attend, and because he has worked a great number of concerts and services, he knows what has worked and failed in the past. He is also willing to try new things; he's not like many promoters who get stuck in a routine."

Besides promoting concerts, Tony is on the Board of Directors for the *SGMA* (Southern Gospel Music Association) *Hall of Fame and Museum*, and works with many organizations, charities and churches.

From an early age Tony has worked in the funeral business as well. Currently he works as a funeral director for *Barney*

Tony with Barney Hampton

Hampton Funeral Service in Boone, North Carolina, and is taking distance-education classes at the *Gupton-Jones College of Funeral Service* in Atlanta, Georgia. He is working on his mortician's degree and is looking forward to completing the courses.

"Tony is friends with a great number of funeral directors, embalmers and morticians across the country," said friend and fellow funeral director, Riley Joe Evans. "We call him 'Digger.' That's an old term for undertaker or mortician that started back in the early western days. Of course, he calls me that, too, but I think it fits him better."

Riley Joe Evans is from Chapmanville, West Virginia, and was one of Tony's groomsmen for his wedding. In fact, Tony had six honorary groomsmen in his wedding — nearly all were funeral directors from around the country.

"It was an honor to be there for Tony;" according to Riley Joe,

"Digger" Greene on the job

"he's been such a wonderful friend over the years ... and to be there with 'Digger' on one of his best days was just great!"

Over the years Tony would stop in and visit local funeral homes while traveling from town to town and state to state, introducing himself as a fellow funeral director. To this day he is a close friend to many of them.

One interesting bit of trivia Tony shares is that Warner Brothers bought the casket and tombstone for their movie *The Green Mile*, which starred Tom Hanks and was filmed nearby, from the funeral home where Tony works. After finishing filming, Warner Brothers gave the casket and tombstone back to the funeral home, which keeps the items as mementos in storage.

With the release of his first comedy recording, *Life's Too Short Not to Laugh*, Tony is quickly becoming recognized as one of the funniest new Christian comedians. He has already done a sequel entitled *Life's Too Short Not to Laugh Again*!

One of the funniest stories about his adventures as a funeral director was the now famous tale he told on the Gaither Homecoming video entitled, *Christmas in the Country*. Tony declared true the story of a woman who asked him to sing three songs at her husband's funeral, and named each of the songs, which included "Jingle Bells". Tony was, of course, puzzled. "Ma'am, I really don't sing 'Jingle Bells' at funerals. Somehow, it just doesn't seem right." The widow clutched his arm and pleaded with him to reconsider and sing the song for it was her husband's favorite. So, after hearing her explanation, he reluctantly agreed.

During the funeral service, when it was time for Tony to sing, he made it through the first two hymns without any problem. He decided that the only way to perform the last song respectfully was to slow it way down, to try to give it more emotion. So, he leaned slightly over the casket and began singing in as serious a tone as he could muster, in his deepest, most somber baritone

voice: "Jin-gle Bells, Jin-gle Bells, Jin-gle all the w-a-y ..." He did his very best to sing it with all of his heart, hoping to please the grieving widow and bring some sort of comfort to the family. As he sang, many of the funeral home guests looked at each another in a rather confused and stunned manner, while several attendees mumbled among themselves. By the time he was finished he was red with embarrassment and wet with perspiration. He then quietly sat down, subtly looked up to the heavens and thanked God the song and the funeral service were finally over.

After the service, Tony walked over to the widow before leaving, and spoke softly, "Ma'am, I surely hope I pleased you and honored your dearly departed." She smiled, nodded and thanked him. Then she added, "But, Tony, I can't believe how mixed up I was earlier."

"Excuse me?" Tony replied.

"Yes, I suppose I am so emotionally and physically exhausted that I'm not thinking too clearly. Tony, I don't know what I was thinkin' ... it wasn't 'Jingle Bells' that was my husband's favorite song — it was 'When They Ring Those Golden Bells!'"

Although many look at Tony as the clown of the family, who is outgoing, loves attention and will do practically anything to make an audience or congregation laugh, he is also a serious, dedicated Christian with a very big heart. He is a smart businessman, as well as a giving man, and has been blessed because of it.

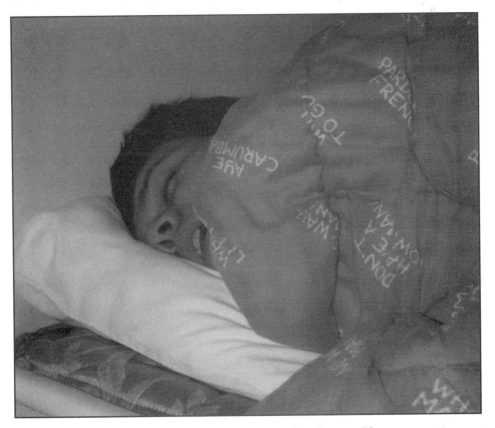

Tony catches up on his rest on the Greenes' bus.

CHAPTER SIX
A SERVANT'S HEART

"Let the rivers run dry, stars will fall
from the sky; still I will be your ser-
vant. I'll keep trusting in you with
everything I do. You're what I live for
— I'm yours."

— Tim Greene, "Let the Rivers Run
Dry," from *At the Cross*

Although Kim Greene grew up with two rough-housing brothers, she was able to conquer any tomboyish mannerisms that she
may have had in her early childhood. She was every bit the prim
and proper little girl who loved dresses, dolls and everything
pretty.

From an early age, she connected with the women in her life
and wanted to be just like them.

"My grandmother owned a hair salon, and I wanted to be a
hairdresser like her and a couple of my aunts," Kim recalls. "I
remember that, even when I was a little girl, all my baby dolls
were bald because I cut off their hair as soon as I got them."

Later in life, Kim enrolled in a course to become a hairdresser,
eventually earning a degree in cosmetology. After graduation, she
worked in her maternal grandmother's shop until the family's
road schedule made it impossible to continue.

"She still keeps her license to this day," Carolyn Greene said of

Tim and Kim

her daughter. "She's always said, 'Momma, I can always sling hair if I have to.'"

"I still do it [cut hair] for the family," Kim said. "With us being on the road so much, and in the public eye, it pays to keep ourselves well-groomed and ready. It also helps me keep up on my work and not forget anything or get rusty."

In addition, Kim has a small clientele of stars who will only allow her to touch their hair.

"Yeah, since we've been working the Gaither concerts, I've been using my skills to help many of the artists we travel with," Kim admitted. "I always do Mr. Gaither's hair before the concerts, and many other artists as well. I've cut hair for Russ Taff, David Phelps, Charlotte Penhollow and even some of the guys on the crew. It keeps me practiced up, and yet it's not really much of a hassle."

Kim has always been fascinated with interior design, as well.

"I'll never forget when I was around sixteen years old, I had saved my money to redesign my bedroom. I remember wanting to cover a whole wall with mirrors, and my mom saying, 'Now, I'm not so sure about this'; but I did, and now, it's probably one of her favorite things about the house today. Interior design is something I still enjoy at my own home."

From an early age, Kim was her Granny Townsend's shadow, giving her a helping hand with whatever she was doing.

"If she was working in the garden, then I was right with her," Kim remembers fondly. "We worked in that old garden so much that when one day someone asked me if I went to kindergarten yet, I answered, 'No, I go to Granny's garden!'"

Snow Townsend was not only the grandmother Kim worked with in the hair salon, but was also Kim's inspiration for singing.

"I sat next to Granny Townsend at every church service," Kim recollected, "and I loved to listen to her sing alto. I wanted to sing alto so bad, so I would sing right with her as best I could. If I didn't sing those notes just right, she'd pop me on the knee and say, 'Nope, this is the way it goes.' So that's honestly where I learned to sing the harmony part — just sitting with her in church."

Kim, Baby Tony and Grandpa "Pop" Clyde Townsend

Although she took part in Girl Scouts, played dress-up and carried baby dolls, singing was Kim's biggest hobby.

"I sang all the time at home," she said. "You couldn't get me to shut up to save my life! I've always just loved singing. I like all kinds of music, but I love Southern Gospel. I grew up listening to the Happy Goodmans, the Hinsons, and the Hoppers when Debra Talley was with them. I learned to mimic all those ladies and learned to open up and let myself become a singer, from singing along with their tapes."

To Kim, singing was a serious matter, and early on she wanted to improve her vocal abilities. That's when she stopped listening as a fan, and began listening as a student.

"Reba Rambo was the biggest influence on me, vocally," she said. "I just loved her voice and range. I also loved the sound the Hinsons had, although not any particular singer; and I also enjoyed listening to Joy Garner from the Downings. But I guess listening to Debra Talley sing with the Hoppers probably helped me more than anything.

"When I was around twelve or thirteen I went through a voice change, like boys do. I had a horrible time singing high notes, so I would listen to the Hopper albums and pay attention to how Debra sang her notes. I remember thinking about how she spoke in such a low voice, but was able to hit the high notes with no problems, and I would think, 'Okay, how is she doing that?' And I would sit for hours mimicking her tones — not as much her style, but her tone placement — and figuring out how I could sing the high notes without hurting myself. So she taught me to sing high and didn't even know it!"

Although music played a primary role in her life growing up, Kim also realized that there was more to family life than just singing, especially growing up as the only girl with two brothers.

"My brothers were tough on me in many ways, yet they were very protective," she said. "Tim and I hardly ever fought, but Tony and I fought like cats and dogs. Tony and I were about seventeen months apart, so we played together, fought together, and cried together. Tony picked on me continuously; he loved nothing better than to pick on me! But then, when we were in school, he always said nobody else better even think about picking on me."

Although childish squabbles and bickering made up much of their youth, as in most families, Kim and her brothers love each other dearly and they share wonderful memories from their childhood.

"I wouldn't trade my relationship with them for anything," she said. "They mean the world to me. We grew up in a close family, and I love that. I hope that someday my children can say the same. Dean (Dean Hopper, Kim's husband) and I have only one child right now, Karlye Jade, but I keep thinking the Lord will give us another one because I'd like for her to experience life with siblings."

Kim ended up going through the same problems Tim had gone through when trying to date while traveling full-time.

"Dating was almost nonexistent," she said. "My parents were strict, and if they didn't approve of the boy I wanted to date, then I just wasn't allowed to date him. The only 'dating' I did was talking to guys at concerts. There were several I would like to have called 'boyfriends,' but because I only got to see them once every two or three months, it just made it impossible.

"Occasionally there were a few

Kim and Tim

guys who cared enough to come visit me at home, and my parents were fine with that as long as they were around. But as far as going out on a date, that just didn't happen — mainly because our schedule made it impossible.

"I had my heart broken several times in high school because the guys I liked couldn't understand why I was gone every weekend. They couldn't understand my lifestyle and that my career was on the road every weekend. The road life kept me from experiencing a normal life, and I envied my high school girlfriends because I wanted a 'normal life', and yet I loved doing what I was doing, and I knew I couldn't have it both ways. So, I came to realize that if I was going to have a boyfriend, he had to be in the industry; otherwise he would not understand my lifestyle."

Dating someone in the industry may have been an alternative, but since singing groups normally randomly schedule their concerts and seldom perform with the same groups, dating other singers or musicians was always a challenge, too.

"I first met Dean Hopper when I was twelve years old," Kim recalls. "My dad had called Claude Hopper (Dean's father) one day and told him about our group and asked Claude if he would listen to us sing sometime. Claude said he would love to hear us, and then told Dad that the

Dean Hopper

Hoppers would be at a tabernacle in Spruce Pines, and for him to bring us over. So, when we got there, Claude asked us to do a few songs to open for them. I don't remember seeing Dean before the concert, but I remember being nervous because they were a professional group.

"Well, the Hoppers got up and sang, and I watched Dean, thinking, 'Oh, he is so cute!' and I immediately had the biggest crush on him. He was seventeen at the time, but with our age difference (about five years) I knew I was too young for him to be interested. I don't even know if he remembers meeting me then."

But it wouldn't take long before Dean took notice of the beautiful young lady Kim was growing into.

"Our families began working together more and more, and we got to know one another well. One day, the Hoppers' bus was in repair, so they borrowed ours while we were off that weekend. Well, Dean made the trek to Boone and spent the night at our house before driving the bus out early the next morning.

"I remember sitting on the couch gnawing on my fingernails because I was so nervous that he was coming to our house. And here I was, all dressed up at ten o'clock at night when he finally showed up!

"He never paid much attention to me until I was around nineteen or twenty. That's when he started calling me on the telephone; and when our families worked together on the road, we would spend time together. I thought he was a nice guy, but I thought he was just playing with me, and that he would end up breaking my heart, so I wouldn't really give him the time of day. Finally, in December of 1987, he called and asked if I wanted to go out on a date during a ski retreat.

"That night while having dinner by candlelight, he looked across the table and said, 'You look beautiful in that light.' I knew right then he was the guy I wanted to spend the rest of my life with. That was in December, and by March of 1988, we were engaged."

Kim's marriage was not a concern for the Greenes, initially, because she never discussed the possibility of leaving the group.

"That was the most difficult time in my life," she now recalls. "Actually, Dean and I talked a lot about how we would work things out after we were married. I knew we were meant for each other, but I couldn't see myself leaving my family. I didn't know how it would work out; I just kept saying, 'Let's just leave it in God's hands.' I guess I was being naive, because you always think love will conquer all."

After a year of traveling on separate buses, Kim realized that love was not conquering the situation.

"I moved to Madison, North Carolina, when we married," Kim said, "and I would drive two and a half hours every week to get on the bus in Boone. Occasionally our families worked together, but we could go a month to six months without seeing each other on the road. Most of the time, Dean was in one bus in one part of the country, and I was on another bus somewhere else. It was so hard for me to adjust, especially in that first year of marriage, where a couple is working hard at getting to know each other.

"So we were together just two days a week before heading back out to what was normal for us. By the time we got back home on Monday, we were like two strangers again. It was like starting over.

"Every Tuesday or Wednesday, when I would have to leave him, I would just cry and cry and cry. It finally came to a point where I was miserable. I knew I could never make the decision to leave my family, so Dean stood up one day and said, 'You can't make this decision, so, as your husband, I'm going to make it for you.'

"So Dean went to my family and explained the situation. He told them that they needed to set a date for a replacement, and that I would help them until they found someone else. He mentioned our love and support for them, but because I was an emotional basket-case, our marriage was suffering."

This was a major happening in the career and lives of the Greenes. They had always been together, and they had always been a close, tight-knit group.

"My family didn't take the news too well at first," Kim recalls. "I think they felt as though I was a traitor or that I was betraying them. They thought I was leaving them and going to another family. I understood their pain, but it didn't make it any easier for me."

"We were devastated — totally devastated," Kim's mother candidly admits. "At that time, Kim was arranging all our songs, and she carried a big load. We were not really sure we could go on without her. We knew it would be tough enough just as a family, much less as a group. We knew that about the only time we would see her would be when our paths crossed on the road.

"But as parents, we wanted her to be happy, and we knew that if that's what it took, then we could accept it and go on."

"When Kim first told us she and Dean were getting married, I think Tim and I knew deep down she would be eventually leaving the group," Tony said. "Mom and Dad refused to believe it, but Tim and I pretty much knew it was just a matter of time.

"Kim and Dean were married at First Baptist Church in Boone, and I'll never forget that day as long as I live. Phil Hoskins married them, and immediately after the couple walked down the aisle as husband and wife, Phil looked at my parents and joked, 'Well, it looks like the Hoppers won!' Hearing this devastated Mom and Dad; Lord, have mercy — they wept like babies."

"It was a tough time for all of us," Kim said. "And I was hoping and praying that God would work it out that we could all somehow work together and stay together, but it was obvious that was not going to happen."

Besides struggling to cope with having to leave the family singing group, Kim was now dealing with homesickness as well.

"When we first married, and I continued to travel with my family, I never had experienced the feeling of leaving home," she said. "But, after I left the group, everything changed. I hardly ever saw my family; I was living in a new home, with a new family and working at a new job. It was a tough couple of years to pull through emotionally, and I sought counseling from pastors and ministers because it was just so hard for me to deal with.

"I had nothing to stand on except the Word of God, and His word says that a man shall leave his father and mother and cleave to his wife, and that she shall leave her family, and they shall cleave one to another; the marriage should come first. So, that's all I had to stand on; to be submissive to my husband and do what he asked me to do."

Kim never doubted that what her husband had asked her to do was in her best interest, and her family even understood that, as well. Yet accepting such change was not easy for any of them.

The pivotal moment came during a Hoppers' recording session for a new album.

"During this time, the Hoppers were struggling with what they were going to do vocally. They couldn't seem to get anything together after trying out a string of new singers, and amid all this they were trying to record a new album. They couldn't get anything to work on this project. They couldn't get the blend they were looking for, and they just felt like nothing was coming together. So they approached me about singing the soprano part on the album because they needed to finish it as soon as possible.

"They were still searching for a new singer, but for now just needed someone to help them finish the recording. They told me that my name didn't have to be on anything, and that no one would have to know that I was singing on the project. So I agreed to help them out.

"I went into the studio, and the first song that I sang with them was 'Here I Am.' The project didn't come out until after I had left the Greenes, but it just so happened that my family heard it months before it was released."

"When we found out that she had recorded with the Hoppers, we knew she was leaving, but that she just didn't want to tell us," Tony said. "It was a hard time for all of us."

"After my family had been given notice that I was leaving the group, my father-in-law approached me about taking the soprano job," Kim said. "He told me if I wanted the job, it was mine, but if I didn't want it, they were going to hire someone else. I told him I wanted it, but I wanted to take several weeks — maybe several months — off the road just to be with my husband.

"Claude agreed, but mentioned a television show they needed to do and asked me if I could help them on it. I hesitated at first, because I didn't want to hurt my family by jumping right into a television show with the Hoppers. I told him that I would do it, but I wanted to talk with my family first. It was a hard thing to do; it really was."

As it turned out, Kim's time off the road was very short.

"They were having a hard time hiring someone temporarily, so I went ahead and started traveling with them sooner than expected," Kim remembers. "At the time I left the Greenes, we had the number one song on the charts: 'When I Knelt the Blood Fell'. The first song I released with the Hoppers, 'Here I Am,' went to number one and was named Song of the Year. In fact, that song was the Hoppers' first number one in their legendary career. So, I took that as God's way of showing me that I was doing what He wanted me to do.

"When I came to the Hoppers, I told the Lord that I didn't want the recognition, and that it was hurtful to even be there at the time. I asked Him to just put me in the background. And do you know that God started using me in ways that I never would have imagined?

"It wasn't long before I started winning awards, and I had never won anything like that before. But I learned that if we seek Him first, and His righteousness, then all these other things will be added.

"I didn't ask for awards; they were actually things I didn't want. But God used them to show me that this is where He wanted me, and that I was not out of His will."

Kim had many doubts when she first left the Greenes, but there was one thing she was certain of: the Greenes would make it without her.

"I think when I left the group, they felt as though they would not be able to make it without me," she said with a broken voice. "But I knew in my heart they could. I knew that they were wonderful singers. I knew that they had been faithful to the Lord and that the Lord was on their side. And I knew beyond a shadow of a doubt that He would take care of them. If I hadn't known that in my heart, I could never have left them."

Later, Tony joked publicly during one of his comedy outings about Kim and Dean's wedding by saying, "Ya'll need to pray for my poor ol' sister Kim; she's backslid and married Dean Hopper — one of *those* Hoppers." The crowd laughed as Tony continued with his outrageously funny routine. Yet, for a short while, the issue was terribly personal and painful for the family. The loss was especially at the forefront of Tim and Tony's thoughts. Their hearts were broken. It was a time of spiritual growth for the Greenes — and growing pains — a season when Christ would again demonstrate His grace and peace.

In time, Tim and Tony found out that rather than losing a sister and precious group member, they gained a wonderful brother-in-law, Dean, and a stronger relationship with the other members of the Hopper family — Claude, Connie, Mike and Denise.

Through the family's total reliance on Christ, the Lord made all things work out for the good. He is forever faithful.

Dean, Kim and daughter, Karlye Jade Hopper
— Photograph by Jonathan Burton Photography, Inc.

The Greenes: Tim, Tony and Amy Lambert

CHAPTER SEVEN
LIFE IS COMPLICATED

"Life is complicated, but there is a
plan to help you in trouble, lend a
helping hand; God's Word is wisdom
and truth, for every man. Life is complicated, but Christ has a plan."

— Tim Greene, "Life Is Complicated,"
from *Whosoever Believes*

Fans at the 1989 National Quartet Convention were unaware Kim was taking the stage as a member of the Greenes for the final time. The audience cheered as the young threesome performed their first number-one, "When I Knelt The Blood Fell".

Midway through the performance, Kim stunned everyone in attendance with an announcement that she was leaving the group, and she told why. Then handing the microphone to a young woman making her way to center stage, Kim walked off the platform. It was the symbolic passing of the torch, and Amy Lambert set the auditorium on fire.

"Amy just walked out there and hit a home run," Tony said. "She instantly brought the crowd to a standing ovation."

The response was a welcome relief for the Greenes.

"All the fans rallied behind us," Tony remembers. "I have to admit, Tim and I thought many times about quitting, but everyone kept saying, 'No, you boys need to keep going; the two of you

have a song to sing and a heart to share. The fans gathered behind us and showed their support. Amy did a great job, and we couldn't have asked for anybody better."

"The first time I heard her sing with Tim and Tony I knew she was the one," Kim recalls. "She sounded great, and with her they still had that Greenes' sound."

"She brought a lot to the group," Everette said. "It was a little different, but she filled the spot beautifully, and the public accepted her as a member."

"Amy is a quiet and passive person," Carolyn added. "And she loves people. She was so easy to travel with, and the Lord knew we needed somebody like that then. Amy knew there was sadness because Kim was gone, and she never tried to take Kim's place; she was just Amy, and she did a wonderful job."

"Amy had a hard row to hoe, though," Tony said. "Everyone compared her to Kim, which wasn't fair because Amy is a fan-

tastic singer in her own right. But because she replaced Kim, she was always searching for acceptance. And I'm sure it was difficult for her, not only with the fans, but also with our family as well. We had never traveled with anyone but family, so it was a real adjustment for all of us."

"It was awkward watching someone else sing in my place," Kim admits. "I remember sitting out in the audience thinking, 'I'm the one that's supposed to be up there with them, not her.' But at the same time, I wanted it to work so badly that I could sit quietly and be supportive. I was their biggest fan — and I still am. More than anything else, whether it was with my voice or someone else's, I wanted the Greenes to succeed."

And Kim did everything she could to help make Amy and the Greenes a success in every way.

"I helped choose Amy," Kim recalls. "I helped train her with everything I knew so the transition would be as easy as possible.

"The following year, Amy won the Singing News Fan Award for Horizon Individual. I took that as a confirmation that I was where God wanted me and Amy Lambert was where He wanted her to be for the time being."

Amy spent her childhood in a little city called Albemarle, North Carolina, with dreams of one day becoming a Gospel singer.

"I grew up in a small church," Amy remembers. "My mom was the pianist, my dad was a deacon, and we were there at church for every service and function. We were there for choir practice, visitation, and to clean the church; it made no difference what was going on; we were there for everything that happened.

"I started singing when I was around three or four years old. Mom sang with a little trio at the church and played piano for them. The church would call on me to sing every once and a while, but I wanted to sing with mom's trio. So, eventually one of the women in the trio left, and I stepped in and started singing her part at the age of seven.

"The name of our trio was The Happy Tones and Amy. The name included 'and Amy' because I was just a little girl, not because I was a star. We began traveling and singing for revivals and conventions in the local area. We did that until I was around sixteen years old. When I started high school, we quit singing, because I was so busy with everything a teenager goes through then."

Although she was no longer singing, Amy never lost her desire to perform; she just needed some time for other things.

"I had wanted to sing professionally since I was seven years old," she recalls. "So everything I did in my life, I did to get to that point. Everything about me had been about getting to sing professionally, because that's all I ever wanted. I didn't want to be anything else, and it's a good thing, because I don't know how to do anything else.

"It's true; I never had the ambition to do anything else. Some kids want to be a nurse or a police officer or something like that; singing was the only thing I ever wanted to do.

"I was seven years old when I went to my first all-night Gospel sing. It was at the Charlotte Coliseum, and I fell in love with it that night. I knew from that moment that this is what I wanted to do with my life. And so from that point, I started working toward reaching that goal."

But an automobile accident left her with outward scars, which brought inward pain and feelings of insecurity. She often wondered if her dreams of becoming a professional singer had been shattered.

"I was staying with my grandmother during the Christmas holidays when I was nine years old," Amy remembers. "My grandmother had an aunt who was a shut-in and didn't get out much, so Grandma would take magazines to her and help around the house. On December 28th, Grandma woke me up and got me

ready to go with her.

"So, we loaded up the car, and I was in the front seat with a stack of magazines. The seat was a bench that stretched from the driver's side to the passenger door. As we started down the hill from her house, the magazines started to slip off the seat. Grandma reached to catch them, and when she did she lost control of the car. She ran off the road and hit a tree. In a split second I was flying through the windshield."

Amy woke up in the hospital with eighty-four stitches in her face, mostly on the right side.

"Every laceration penetrated all seven layers of skin," she explains. "It pulled all the gums from my teeth, and my eyelids were cut through, as were my lips. I also suffered internal injuries, but the cuts and tears were the worse. It took them over two-and-a-half hours to sew up my face.

"For several days they would not allow me to look in a mirror. But I found one on the serving tray one day and took a look, and my life has not been the same since. The first thing I remember saying to my parents was, 'Nobody will ever love me like this.'"

After leaving the hospital, Amy had to suffer the worst of her traumatic experiences while attending school. Children can often be unfair and cruel.

"The other kids made fun of me and called me names," she remembered. "They called me Cut-lip, Scar-face and many other horrible names. It seemed every day my mother was going to school with the intent of spanking some child for verbal abuse.

"But adults were just as bad. People would just stare at me and say, 'What happened to you? Did you get bit by a dog, or did you run into a barbed wire fence?' At nine years old, it was hard for me to get over people staring at me like I was a freak or something."

Even though she went through six reconstructive surgeries, Amy still felt different from everyone around her. She struggled with loneliness and discontentment, but eventually found peace and a sense of belonging after placing her faith and trust in Jesus Christ.

"My mother told me something that helped me more than anything," Amy remembers. "She said, 'Amy, don't you ever be ashamed to stand up in front of people and tell them about Jesus. Remember, He has scars in his hands and in His feet, and it was all for you. He wasn't ashamed of you when He raised His hands and died on Calvary.' And there is never a moment that I'm standing in front of a crowd that I don't think of that."

It was Amy's own longing for peace as a child that led her into a life of ministry for others.

"There are so many hurting people who need ministered to," she said. "I believe God has allowed me to experience pain in certain areas of my life so I could understand the pain of others and help them in some small way. I have experienced things in my life that only the Lord could have brought me through. And if I hadn't leaned on Jesus during those times, I would never be happy today."

Amy worked at a television station in Greenville, South Carolina, before joining the Greenes. She had all but forgotten her dreams of singing professionally.

"I was talking with Tim Riley one day at a Gold City concert," Amy remembers. "He asked me what I was doing, and when I told him, he said I should be singing. I told him that I would love to, but there just wasn't a place for me, that openings for female singers were few and far in between. I said, 'There are just no jobs coming open.' And he said, 'I know of one coming open.'

"I asked him what he was talking about and he told me about Kim marrying Dean. He mentioned that he felt she would soon have to decide whether to stay with her family or move on with the Hoppers. Tim said he thought I would be a perfect replacement for Kim.

"I didn't think much about it because the Greenes and Hoppers made it well known publicly that Kim would continue to sing and travel with the Greenes, and Dean would continue to sing and travel with his family. I just put that conversation out of my mind because I had had too many "almost" opportunities, and I didn't want another let-down."

Because Amy booked groups for concerts for the television station, it was not unusual for groups or artists to call her at work. So she didn't think much about it when someone told her Tony Greene was on the line for her.

"I had no idea why Tony was calling," Amy said. "I answered the phone and soon found out. He mentioned that he had talked with Tim Riley, who had told him of my interest in a job if Kim ever left. He then said, 'I think Kim is going to leave. Can you come to Boone and audition?'

"So I drove to Boone and auditioned, and everything fell into place. I think we were all a little shocked at how well we blended. And that's how I knew that's where God wanted me to be. He made everything fit so perfectly; everything just fit like a puzzle, and we knew it."

Before making a decision, the Greenes wanted to take Amy on the road for a few weekends to see how it worked out.

"During this time I was trying not to get excited and get my hopes up because I just didn't want to be let down again. I knew in my heart this was where God wanted me, but I just didn't want to be hurt again. So I traveled some dates with them and they finally hired me with the understanding that if Kim changed her mind, the job would no longer be available. I understood that, but I think in their heart of hearts, they did not think Kim would actually ever leave them.

"That was a painful week for the Greenes. There were many rumors going around, and so many groups knew me from the TV station and asked why I was at the National Quartet Convention

Dining during a Gospel music cruise is, seated, Amy Lambert, Tim and wife, Amy, Tony (standing) and Carolyn and Everette Greene.

with the Greenes. I couldn't say anything, and the Greenes wouldn't say anything, so it was a huge secret that was getting ready to come out.

"We practiced once that week for about forty-five minutes. Then I waited for Kim to announce my name from the stage, at which point I went out and sang the second verse of 'When I

The Greenes: Tim, Tony and Melina Parks

Knelt The Blood Fell' in front of ten thousand fans.

"That was the most incredible experience of my life. I have never had a moment since that would compare. There were cameras going off everywhere, and afterwards, the room where singers get ready before going onstage was filled with singers and industry people shaking my hand and taking pictures. I didn't realize it at the time, but it was history in the making."

Then, unfortunately for the Greenes, in 1994 they found themselves conducting another search for a soprano singer after Amy met her future husband-to-be, Jeff Templeton, and decided a solo career would give her more time to spend with him.

Kim gave Tim and Tony the phone number of a young woman from Cumming, Georgia, named Milena Parks.

"I had filled in for the Hoppers while Kim was out with laryngitis once," Milena recalls. "So when the Greenes asked Kim if she knew of someone to replace Amy, she told them about me. She told them that I might be interested in filling in, but she wasn't sure if I would want the job full time.

"So they called on a Wednesday night, asking me to come to Wilkesboro, North Carolina, the following night to sing with them that weekend. I wound up traveling with them for three weekends straight, and after they auditioned a few other singers, they offered me the position in June of that year."

Like Amy, singing Gospel music professionally had also been a dream of Milena's since childhood.

"Since I was a teenager, I knew that's what I wanted to do," she said. "I never thought it would happen, but I was twenty-two when it did, and it was just a dream come true. Just to get to sing with a group I grew up listening to was unbelievable.

"I remember listening to the Greenes live 10th Anniversary cassette so many times that I knew every song on it backwards and forwards. I grew up loving their music and loving their harmonies, and it just amazes me that God allowed me to sing with them and become good friends with them."

Milena was no stranger to singing when she made her professional debut filling in for Kim with the Hoppers in 1991. She grew up singing with her sisters, April and Rebecca, as a trio in their hometown of Cumming.

"I started singing with my sisters when I was six years old,"

Milena remembers. "We performed the traditional convention music styles, like the Stamps-Baxter School of Music and the Georgia School of Music. We sang Southern Gospel in our local churches, including revivals and special performances.

"We performed together until I was around sixteen, when my oldest sister married, and then we just performed weddings, funerals and special events."

Milena's love for music was obvious at an early age.

"My mother always said that I would sit on the front steps of our porch and sing to my baby dolls before I could even talk," Milena recalls. "There was a little boy in our neighborhood, and he and I would play 'church' everyday. He would preach and I would sing. So singing Gospel music stuck with me the rest of my life."

Although she had a different personality than either Kim or Amy, Milena was a good fit for the Greenes.

"Each group member has been the perfect person for the time they were with us," Carolyn said. "Where Amy was quiet and passive, Milena was always bubbly, happy and just a wonderful person. She kept everyone laughing and was always fun to be around."

"She is so much the extrovert," like-minded Tony said with a laugh. "She is outgoing and funny, and we always had a great time with her."

"I had so much fun traveling with the Greenes," Milena said. "I laughed more on that bus than I ever thought was possible. Tony and I were always joking and cutting up, of course, but Tim was, too. I know everyone thinks of Tim as quiet and shy, but he clowned around as much as the rest of us. I can honestly say that in the time I spent with the Greenes, there was never a dull moment!"

The behind-the-scenes atmosphere translated to the stage and public in general.

"I'll never forget the time we were in Seminole, Oklahoma, with the Hoppers at the big Seminole Sing," Milena said. "I was standing at the product table talking with Claude Hopper when a woman came over to buy a tape. She was a sweet little old woman who looked every bit the perfect granny. She looked at me and said, 'I enjoyed your singing tonight, but I wanted to know, what happened to that skinny girl?' She was talking about Amy Lambert, of course, and off the top of my head I just said, 'She's not with the group anymore; I ate her!' I thought Claude was going to fall over laughing. He told me later he'd never heard a comeback like that; I told him that I know I'm not the smallest thing in the world, but she caught me totally off guard!"

Milena had many influences in the Gospel music industry, and she has taken much from all of them.

"When I was growing up, the Nelons were popular and I would sit on Sunday mornings and listen to them sing on TV," she remembers. "I realized that that is what I wanted to do, too."

She says the Hoppers, the Perrys, and the Talleys have also influenced her.

"Just about every group with a female singer has made an impact on my style of singing at one time or another," she said. "The Greenes were especially influential upon me when Kim was with them as I was growing up."

When Milena made the difficult decision to leave the Greenes in 1997, Tim and Tony wondered if the revolving door to the soprano position would ever stop. But just around the corner, God was preparing another vocalist for such a time as this.

The Greenes: Tim, Tony and TaRanda Kiser

CHAPTER EIGHT
WEDDING SONG

A Daisy

A daisy is a flower that's never sad,
It's always happy, always glad.

It brings sunshine to a rainy day,
And takes away the awful gray.

A daisy is something never to let go,
It makes you feel special, and your
heart aglow.

So pick a daisy and hold it tight,
And your life will be filled with a
meaningful light.

TaRanda Kiser was born April 6th, 1979, and grew up traveling with her musical family, the Kisers, who sang locally in and around St. Petersburg, Florida.

However, because their area was more acclimated to contemporary Christian music, the Kisers were not too familiar with Southern Gospel or the artists performing it.

"I guess I'd probably heard of the Greenes," TaRanda recalls.

"But I had never heard them in concert or knew any of the songs they recorded."

She may not have been familiar with the Greenes or Southern Gospel music, but TaRanda knew great songs when she heard them.

"As a Gospel group, we nearly lived in the local music store looking for sound tracks to sing," she said. "One day I found a song called 'When I Knelt, the Blood Fell,' and we fell in love with it. We had no idea the Greenes had recorded the song, but we loved it."

When Milena Parks decided to leave the group in 1997, the Greenes found themselves again searching for a soprano replacement.

"That was a rough time for all of us," Tony recalls. "We also found out that Tim's mother-in-law, Shirley Vernor, had a malignancy in her liver. It was an extremely troubling time for Tim's wife, Amy, and he wanted to be there for her. 'Miss Shirley' only lived three weeks after doctors discovered the cancer.

"The night we had scheduled to be in Waycross, Georgia, she was at the point of death. Tim, of course, was with Amy at Miss Shirley's bedside.

"Milena and I called a friend, Tony Jarmon, to go with us and sing Tim's part. Jarmon, of course, has performed with Phil Cross and Poet Voices and Legacy Five, and is now a solo artist.

"Well, Tony Jarmon met us in Charlotte, North Carolina, and I'll never forget how nervous I was — I'm not kidding, I was on pins and needles. I had performed without Kim and Dad many times, but I had never walked on a stage without my brother Tim. And when they announced 'The Greenes' it was so weird because it was actually 'The Greene'; I was the only Greene out there!"

***

Meanwhile, at one of the low points in their lives, Tim, Amy and others gathered near Miss Shirley's bedside for her last solemn moments on earth. As the family sang "Amazing Grace," Amy's dear mother met Jesus face to face and entered into His heavenly kingdom.

When Tim later did his second solo project, the *In His Eyes* video, he talked about his close relationship with "Miss Shirley" and sang a song he composed about her, entitled, "Come Away, My Love," based upon verses from Song of Solomon.

> My beloved spake, and said unto me, Rise up, my love, my fair one, and come away. For, lo, the winter is past, the rain is over and gone ...
>
> — Song of Solomon 2:10-11, KJV

"She was a very special woman, and we still miss her a great deal," Tim expressed. "Yet, we delight and are consoled in knowing that we will see and be with her again."

> The LORD is my shepherd; I shall not want. He maketh me to lie down in green pastures: He leadeth me beside the still waters. He restoreth my soul: He leadeth me in the paths of righteousness for His name's sake. Yea, though I walk through the valley of the shadow of death, I will fear no evil: for Thou art with me; Thy rod and Thy staff they comfort me. Thou preparest a table before me in the presence of

mine enemies: Thou anointest my head with oil; my cup runneth over. Surely goodness and mercy shall follow me all the days of my life: and I will dwell in the house of the LORD forever.

— Psalm 23, KJV

***

There were more reasons for Tony's anxieties than that of Tim not being with him during this period.

"We were late getting to the concert and a storm was brewing when we pulled into the parking lot," he recalls. "It was getting ready to rain cats and dogs; I mean it was one of those Southern Georgia 'toad stranglers.' I was trying to get our product table and equipment inside when a young woman walked up and introduced herself."

"I had met Kim and the Hoppers the week before," TaRanda said. "And Kim told me that Milena was leaving the Greenes and that I should send a demo to Tony and Tim. Well, we had no idea how to make a demo, so we called a friend at our local television station and asked if he could help us shoot video for a demo. So instead of just gathering around a piano and singing, like most singers do in a demo, we ended up with a top-notch, high-quality videotape."

"She came up to me as I am trying to wrestle with the equipment and get everything ready," Tony recalls, "and says, in a bouncy, cheery tone, 'Hi! I'm TaRanda Kiser; I met your sister, Kim, last week, and she told me to come introduce myself and give you a demo.'

"I really, really tried to be cordial, but my nerves were already

TaRanda Kiser

shot, so I thanked her and continued what I was doing," Tony recalled.

TaRanda had entered a talent show held prior to the Greene concert and was waiting to hear who had won, so she was especially nervous as well. When she later learned she had won the contest, she was overwhelmed with joy.

"I was so excited about winning that I forgot to give Tony the demo later," she remembers. " I didn't really want to give it to him in front of Milena anyway, because it just seemed a little awkward, knowing she was leaving the group and all."

The following week, TaRanda called the Greenes' office, asking where Tony wanted her to send the demo.

"She told me how she forgot to give me the videocassette while at the Waycross sing," Tony said. "I asked her if she could 'overnight' it to our office, and she said she could.

"The tape arrived the next day, and I watched it with my parents. We couldn't believe what we were hearing. The first song she sang on the tape was 'When I Knelt The Blood Fell,' and it was just awesome."

"What's amazing is that when we recorded that demo, I had no idea that it was a Greenes song, or that Tim had written it," TaRanda added. "It was just my favorite to sing, and my family had more requests to perform it than any other song on our list."

"We were all blown away by the demo," Tony said. "After listening to the first two songs, I remember saying that she was definitely the one we were looking for and that we needed to let Tim see the tape. Momma looked at me and said, 'If you hire that girl, you'll end up marrying her!'"

"That's because I was so sweet and ravishing on the video," TaRanda said facetiously, with a laugh.

"Yeah, right," Tony said, rolling his eyes and trying not to smile. "The video was out of this world, but when she came to Boone for an audition she was sick. Remember, she was from Florida, and it was November in Boone, which means it was cold with snow and ice.

"We were auditioning other singers as well, so we had our hands full. We held auditions at our church, and we had all the applicants stay in their cars until we were ready for them.

"Even though she was under the weather, we felt TaRanda was the best we'd heard. In fact, we were amazed at the blend we had on the very first try. So, we asked her to go on the road with us

Tony, TaRanda, Dennis Swanberg, and Tim on *Swan's Place*

and see how everything went. After three weeks of road testing, she was officially hired. That was Thanksgiving night in 1997, and we sang at the Tennessee Theater in Knoxville, Tennessee."

It appeared as though God's hand was in the mix for everyone involved, despite TaRanda's nervousness about singing publicly with Tim and Tony for the first time, knowing what all this could mean for her career.

"I'm still astonished at how everything came together," Tony said. "After we hired TaRanda, we brought her mom and dad on the bus and told them our plans. Of course, they were thrilled; they just sat and cried because it was always TaRanda's dream to sing professionally.

"And it was amazing how God worked everything out, because they lived in Florida, but her dad suddenly got a transfer to Knoxville, Tennessee."

"A transfer he had applied for four years prior," TaRanda added.

"So, it worked out well," said Tony. "In fact, her family had moved to Knoxville before we had even hired her. That was God working everything out, because Knoxville is only a three-hour drive from Boone."

TaRanda made a big splash with audiences everywhere. The blend of harmonies she brought was reminiscent of the days when Kim traveled with the group. However, TaRanda also brought a new energy and excitement to the group.

As Amy Lambert said recently, "TaRanda sounds more like Kim than Milena or I ever did. She has been so good for the group."

"Amy had the tones on the high notes like me," Kim recalls. "But I don't think we sounded that much alike. People always tell me that TaRanda and I sound so much alike. I take that as a great compliment because I think she is a phenomenal singer."

Just as it was with every soprano following Kim, people won-

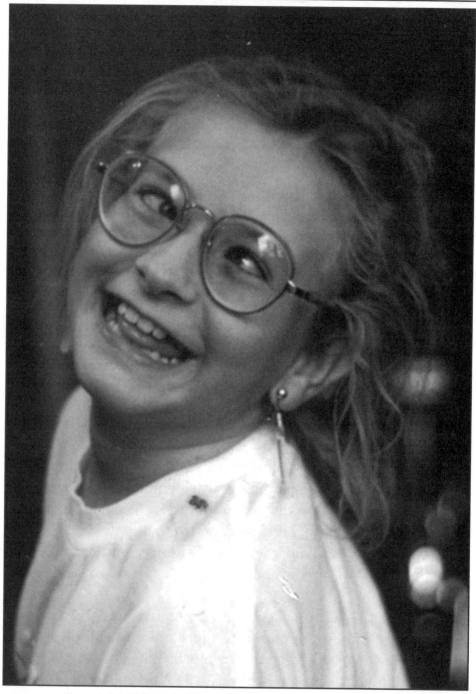

As a child, TaRanda Kiser clowns around for the camera.

dered if Tony and TaRanda would become a couple.

"I kept thinking Tony would eventually find a wife through all the personnel changes," Kim said. "Every time they hired someone new, I wondered if she was the one. TaRanda wasn't with them six months before I knew she and Tony would someday marry. I don't think he even knew it at that point, but I knew she was the one for him."

"The more we traveled on the bus together, the more I realized that TaRanda liked me a lot," Tony said with a sneaky grin. "She was attracted to me."

"It's true," TaRanda said. "I let him know about my interest, but he would never give it a second thought, because he was terrified of what effects a relationship could have."

"Well, it was like the TV show, *The Nanny*," Tony said. "You've got Mr. Sheffield, who is the boss, and then you have Fran Drescher, who is the nanny. Well, I was the boss and TaRanda was the employee, and I was scared of how it could turn out."

"Are you saying I look like Fran Drescher?" TaRanda teased.

"No-o-o-o," Tony said with a laugh. "You know what I'm saying."

"No, he was just scared, and I understand," TaRanda said. "He worried if the relationship didn't

TaRanda and Tony

work out, he could also lose a singer. There was a lot to consider with it. But I just knew early on that this was meant to be. I knew there was a reason, other than just being on the road singing, that God put us together."

However, Tony had just come out of a painful relationship and wasn't looking for a commitment.

"The funny thing about it is that his ex-girlfriend was my hairdresser," TaRanda said with a big smile. "She was always talking about her boyfriend, and after a few appointments I realized she was talking about Tony Greene!"

"We had dated for about three years," Tony added, seeming somewhat embarrassed.

"Well, Tim's daughter, Brittany, was my little spy," TaRanda said with a giggle. "She was around seven or eight years old, and would tell me what was going on in Tony's love life. One day she came on the bus all excited and said, 'You're not going to believe this; Tony and his girlfriend broke up! They are history forever!' So that's when I decided to make my move.

"I said, 'Tony, I know you just broke up with your girlfriend, but I'd like to talk to you, to see if you feel there would ever possibly be a relationship between us.' I left it at that, and I really thought he just wasn't interested."

TaRanda stayed at Everette and Carolyn's house on Sunday nights if the bus pulled in too late for her to drive to Knoxville. Tony still lived at home with his parents, so one night after Everette and Carolyn went to bed, TaRanda told Tony she wanted to talk to him.

"I said, 'You know I have these feelings for you, and I know you have feelings for me, too, because I feel it. I just want to know what the deal is — why you won't pursue this.' His eyes got big as baseballs, his face turned red, and he whispered, 'My mom and dad are in the next room! Can we not talk about this right now?' I told him we didn't have to talk about it then, but sooner or later we were going to have to."

"Not long after that, TaRanda and I traveled to Joy FM radio station in Winston-Salem, North Carolina, to promote our Jubilee-on-the-Mountain event," Tony remembers.

Tony and TaRanda stylin' at a Halloween party

"He woke me up at four o'clock in the morning and asked if I wanted to go with him," TaRanda continues. "He said, 'I think we can talk on the way back home.' So, I thought, 'All right! Finally, he's going to tell me how he feels.' But the whole trip back, he didn't say anything! Not one word. Then, just two miles away from Boone, he said, 'So, what did you want to talk about?'"

"Then I finally told her that I thought that maybe it would be a good idea to start seeing each other," Tony said.

"But we decided we would keep it all under wraps," TaRanda said. "We would date privately and see where it would go. Nobody knew we were seeing each other, not even his mom and dad; I think Tim probably had an idea because he was on the bus with

us, but we told no one."

"We made it a secret because if it didn't work out, we didn't want our friends and fans to have the wrong impression of things," Tony said. "But there wasn't a night on the road that someone didn't tell us that we were made for each other, or that I better not let her get away.

"So we had dated a year before I settled in my heart that TaRanda was the woman I wanted to spend the rest of my life with. I always called her 'Daisy' and she called me 'Buck'. Well, every night before we would hang up the telephone, she would say, 'I love you, Buck; I wear a size six.' She was talking about her ring size, of course, and I would always say, 'Why, your foot ain't that big!'"

"By that time all our close friends knew we were dating," TaRanda said.

"They knew because TaRanda couldn't keep her mouth shut," Tony said jokingly. "You know how girls are ... they're gonna talk — they've gotta talk!"

By now Tony was planning the next step in their relationship.

"Nick Holland came to Boone a day before we headed out to the National Quartet Convention," Tony remembers. "We went around Boone looking for a ring for TaRanda. So, I found the one I liked and bought it. Yes, it was a size six, and TaRanda didn't have a clue that I'd bought it.

"Nick was the only person who knew I was going to pop the question. I didn't even tell my parents or her parents what I was planning; I didn't tell anyone."

"I had no idea he was planning anything," TaRanda said. "No idea whatsoever."

"We were scheduled to sing Thursday at the National Quartet Convention, so Wednesday night I got her dad away from everyone to talk. I told him that I loved his daughter with all my heart and I wanted his permission to ask her to marry me. I asked him not to tell anyone, and that what we talked about was to be confidential. I had no more got up from the table, when he went straight and told his wife, and she went straight and told Daisy, 'He's going to ask you to marry him! Don't say anything; he just talked to your dad. I don't know when he's going to do it, but he's going to do it!'

"Later that night I decided to take TaRanda to a late-night dinner. I took her to Ruth's Chris Steak House; that's one of our favorite places to eat. It has a romantic atmosphere and from the top of the building, you can see the skyline of Louisville. Well, TaRanda thought that I had brought her there to pop the question."

"I was so nervous," she recalls. "I couldn't eat a bite."

"And I sat there and ate like a pig and just talked," Tony went on, "but never said a word about marriage. She was as mad as a hornet because I didn't ask her that night."

"Oh, I was; I was fuming," TaRanda said with a laugh. "We started to leave and I said, 'Well, is that it? Is there anything else you want to talk about?'"

"So the next day I went to a local flower shop and bought her a bouquet of daisies and hid them in the back of my car with the ring. Nobody knew about this except my bus driver, Greg Crow, Nick Holland and Kirk Talley."

Tony's plan was to propose to Daisy while onstage that night at the National Quartet Convention.

"I asked one of the Convention board members, Charlie Burke, if I could take one minute after our time onstage to ask Daisy to marry me. He said I could, so those were the only four people who knew."

"I was good friends with Kirk Talley's table workers, and they asked me what was going to happen that night during our set," TaRanda recalls. "And I said that I didn't know. I never dreamed he would propose on the NQC stage; after all, we had kept everything so private. The women said, 'Well, something is going to happen because Kirk told us we wouldn't want to miss it.' I told them I had no idea what it could be, and I honestly never dreamed he was cooking this up."

"When we got to the Convention Center, I gave the ring to my bus driver, Greg," Tony said. "And he took the flowers to the auditorium and hid them under the stage."

"So, during this time, I am upset with Tony because we were

late getting to the Singing News Fan Awards," TaRanda remembers. "He would not get moving and I was saying, 'Come on, we're going to be late!' and he was over to the side talking with his mom. I later found out he was advising her to be at the stage when we performed, that he was going to ask me to marry him. That was the first time she knew anything about our relationship. He knew that we would not be back in time to give her the news before we went on."

After the Awards Ceremony, the Greenes were to perform second in the lineup on the main stage.

"Karen Peck was after us and was waiting backstage," TaRanda said. "And Tony told her before we went onstage to not let me leave the area because he had an announcement to make. So after we sang, I'm trying to hurry to get back to our table when Karen walks up to me and starts talking. Every time I start to walk away, she complimented me on something. First, it was my dress, and then it was my necklace, hair and shoes.

"Meanwhile, Tony is still onstage talking to the crowd. I didn't even hear what he was saying; all I wanted to do was get back to the table. Suddenly he said, 'Daisy, come out here for a minute,' and I had no idea what was going on. He took my hand and said, 'TaRanda and I have been dating for about a year now,' and I thought, 'Oh, my gosh, his mom is going to kill us!' but I still had no clue what he was doing; I thought he was just breaking the news to everyone that we were dating.

"And then he said, 'Daisy, I just want you to know that I love you, and I want to spend the rest of my life with you.' I was so embarrassed in front of all those people; all I wanted to do was to get off the stage. Then he said, 'There's just one more thing,' and he got the ring and flowers, and I had no idea what he was doing until I turned around and saw him on his knee."

"I did it just like in the movies," Tony said. "I got down on one knee and with a bouquet of daisies in one hand and the ring in the other, I said, 'Daisy, will you marry me?' She said 'yes,' and then I gave her the ring."

"I don't think I said 'yes,'" TaRanda said with a laugh. "I think I was just crying."

"Yeah, you were just bawling. Anyway, she shook her head 'yes,' and that was the cue for the soundman to play 'What A Wonderful World' by Louis Armstrong. And that's what was playing when we walked off the stage. That was a special night that I will never forget."

"Of course, we had thousands of people waiting for us at our table," TaRanda recalls. "They were taking pictures, hugging us and giving congratulations."

"It was neat," Tony said with a smile. "Tim and I grew up at the Convention, and these people grew up with us. Southern Gospel music fans are such a close-knit bunch that our fans feel as though they are part of our family, so they were there to share the moment with us."

Plans for the wedding began immediately.

"I wanted to go ahead and have the wedding at Christmas, but Daisy wouldn't do it," Tony said. "It was September, and she said she didn't have enough time."

"Well, especially the way we were on the road all the time," TaRanda said. "Our schedule had us on the West Coast the first two weeks of December, and he wanted to marry at Christmas! I told him that I couldn't be away from home for two solid weeks and then come home and get married. So we picked the next red holiday."

"We set the date for February 13th, 2001. We couldn't set it for the fourteenth because we were already committed to do a Homecoming video shoot with Bill Gaither in Asheville, North Carolina. It was a shot at The Cove, which is the Billy Graham Training Center.

"We ended up on a three-week tour of the West Coast, and

TaRanda was a handful! She was on the road trying to plan a wedding, and had everybody doing stuff for her."

"We were planning the flowers; we were planning the invitations and the colors; I mean, we were doing everything from the road!" TaRanda remembered.

"The worst three weeks of my life was on that bus trying to plan a wedding," Tony said in jest, shaking his head.

"And he had no interest in helping *at all*," TaRanda said, rolling her eyes. "He'd just say, 'Whatever. That sounds good to me.'"

"But it all worked out," Tony said. "We had a lot of help from the folks at our church. Tim and I've always attended Westview Baptist, and they have always been family to us. All the women of the church jumped in and helped us with all the details."

"There is no way we could have had the wedding without our church family," TaRanda said. "No way."

"They did everything," Tony added. "The flowers, decorating, food and catering — they did it all. Grandma Tressie Greene owned a flower shop and took care of the floral arrangements. My mom and Velva Fancher did all the coordinating and all the food.

"They asked me if I had any special requests, and the only request I had was to have Chick-fil-A nuggets at our reception — that's all I asked for."

"But, there isn't a Chick-fil-A in Boone," TaRanda said with a smile. "However, they have a small one on the campus of Appalachian State for the students. So, we had to put in a special request for the kitchen to make however many thousands of nuggets that were needed."

"We needed a lot because we sent out probably six hundred invitations," Tony said.

"I wanted to have a sit-down R.S.V.P. reception, because I think those are so elegant," TaRanda added. "But *Tony* got on Joy FM radio while we were sending out invitations, and invited everybody!"

"Well, I didn't know any better," he said meekly, in his defense. "Everybody was calling in and talking about it, and I just went on the air and said, 'Lord, why don't all y'all come?'"

"He did!" TaRanda said. "He just couldn't stop either. He said, 'Now don't forget it's the *thirteenth*, and *you don't have to R.S.V.P. or anything*. You just come on and join us!' I couldn't believe he was doing it."

"Boy, I sure got my ears lowered when I got home, I'll tell you that," Tony said, with a sheepish grin.

"We couldn't do anything structured because we had no idea how many people were coming," TaRanda said.

"Yeah, but it turned out so nice," Tony added. "They pulled it together so well and everything was great."

"That's true," said TaRanda. "Everybody did a great job."

"But the night of the wedding was a cold, rainy, foggy, nasty night," Tony remembers. "It wasn't snowing, but snow was on the ground. I'll never forget; I had Paul Oglesby bring a limousine from the funeral home where I worked. So instead of renting a limo, I had the family car from the funeral home — because it didn't cost anything!"

"We were riding around in the back with the smell of funeral carnations," TaRanda said with a laugh.

"Paul came by the house and picked up all the guys," Tony said. "I invited three of my best friends to stand up with me. My best friend in the whole world is Jamey Hodges, so I asked him, Greg Douglas and Andy Thompson to be part of the ceremony. Jamey's mother became critically ill about three weeks before the wedding and so he couldn't make it. She was in MD Anderson Hospital in Dallas, Texas, receiving treatment at the Cancer Center. So we went ahead with the other two, and I also had six honorary groomsmen with me."

"We should have called them the six honorary *pallbearers*,"

TaRanda said, with a laugh.

"Yeah, that's true," Tony agreed. "The whole front pew was full of mostly funeral directors. My honorary groomsmen were my brother, Ronnie Brookshire, Barney Hampton, Greg Hampton, Riley Joe Evans, Rob Johnson and Tim Brooks, who recently passed away."

"They were all funeral directors, except for Ronnie," TaRanda said.

"They all wore black suits, white shirts and red ties," Tony elaborated.

"Our colors were red and black," TaRanda said. "Now the two that stood with Tony wore tuxedos that matched his. I had two girls, who wore gowns that were a dual-tone red. I also had honorary bridesmaids, who were all sisters-in-law. They all wore black dresses and carried a single red rose."

At first it looked like things were not going to go off as smoothly as they had hoped the day of the wedding.

"For starters, the woman we hired to do TaRanda's hair before the wedding was late getting there," Tony recalls.

"I had paid her around six hundred dollars to do my hair and makeup," TaRanda said. "In fact, she was to do hair and makeup for all the women in the wedding. She came up from Winston-Salem, North Carolina, and I paid for her hotel and gave her gas and food money as well. I did it because I trusted her to do a good job; I didn't want to worry about my hair or makeup, so I hired a professional."

"By the time she had done all the other girls, though, she only had a few minutes left to do mine! She didn't have time to do the hairstyle I had originally picked, so we went with something simple and quick. I was a nervous wreck!

"We were five or ten minutes late getting started," Tony said. "But once it started, everything fell into place. We did things a little differently in the ceremony; we had bagpipes playing

'Amazing Grace' while I walked down the aisle with my daddy on one arm and my momma on the other.

"My brother Tim married us, and our friends, Phil Cross, Donnie Henderson, Richie Works and Robert Matthews took care of the music during the ceremony," Tony said.

"They did a great job," TaRanda added.

"The ceremony lasted twenty minutes or less," Tony said. "And then we went over and had a big time at the reception. Everything was going well until they told us to cut the cake and feed it to each other. While holding the piece of cake up to TaRanda's mouth, I watched in horror as it broke apart, and some of it fell straight down onto TaRanda's chest!"

"It went right down inside the neckline of my dress," TaRanda said, laughing. "But instead of letting it go for the pictures, without thinking, Tony started digging his hand down into my dress, just trying to be helpful and get the cake out!"

"Lord, everybody started screaming and laughing," Tony

TaRanda, Tony (wearing his "Bubba" teeth) and Carolyn Greene

laughed. "That just embarrassed me to death!"

"But he honestly didn't realize what it looked like," TaRanda said. "He was really just trying to get the cake out for me."

"We probably had over five hundred people there," Tony remembers. "We stood in line and greeted them all; and we had so many gifts ... I mean hundreds of gifts. Our friends took all of the gifts home for us, and the limousine took TaRanda and me back to my house. When we got to the house, TaRanda had rice all over her."

"Everybody — especially my ornery brothers — pelted us with rice when we came out of the church," TaRanda said. "It was everywhere!"

"We were dead tired when we got to the house," Tony said. "It was around twelve-thirty or one o'clock in the morning, and we still had to change our clothes and drive two hours to Asheville,

North Carolina, to our motel before getting up at eight o'clock in the morning to do a Gaither video.

"So when we got home, we were rushing to change clothes and get on the road. I went into the bedroom to change clothes, and TaRanda went into the garage because her dress had rice all down inside it, and she didn't want to get it all over the house. Well, she got out there and couldn't unfasten all those little hooks in the back by herself, so she hollered for me to come help her undo her dress."

"And he wouldn't do it!" TaRanda interrupted.

"No, I wouldn't do it!" Tony said, seriously. "I said, 'I ain't agonna do that!' and TaRanda said, 'But, Tony, we're married,' and I said, 'Still, it just ain't right!' Thank God, her momma pulled into the driveway at that very moment!"

"My mom had to come in and help me undo the gown!" TaRanda said.

"Lord, I was so embarrassed; I would have died if I had to do that!" Tony said, laughing about it now.

"I thought I was going to have to wear that wedding gown all

the way to Asheville," TaRanda mumbled sarcastically.

"By the next morning, when we showed up at the Cove for the video shoot, I had forgotten how ruthless our friends on the Gaither tour could be," Tony said. "All they talked about the whole time was us newlyweds, our honeymoon, and stuff like that. Between songs Bill Gaither would look back at us and say, 'Is everything all right back there?' Everybody would look at us, and we'd blush. They'd do anything to embarrass us."

"Russ Taff was catcalling," TaRanda said with a laugh. "So was Lynda Randle and...well, everybody was getting into the act!"

"Everybody had something to say," Tony added. "Well, after we finished the video shoot, we went back into Asheville to get something to eat at Chili's restaurant. We were so dead tired that Daisy fell asleep at the restaurant!"

— Photograph by Jonathan Burton Photography, Inc.

By later that week, technically speaking, the Greenes were back on the road traveling again as a family for the first time in eight years. It was truly "the Greenes" again. The marriage had come at the perfect time. Tony would later realize having TaRanda's love and support would be vital in surviving the challenges that lay ahead. For Tony and TaRanda, this was a marriage made in Heaven.

Carolyn Townsend's baptism

"Pop" Clyde Townsend during World War II

Tony, Carolyn and Kim

Tim, Tony and Kim

Tim, Kim and Tony

Tim, beside Dad, Everette, holding Kim and Tony

Kim

Tim

Tim, Everette, Kim and Carolyn

Tim Greene

A young Ronnie Brookshire

Tony (left) and Kim dress up for Halloween

Is this Ben & Jerry, or Tim and Tony?

The Loft recording studio is a humble dwelling with
state-of-the-art recording technology inside.

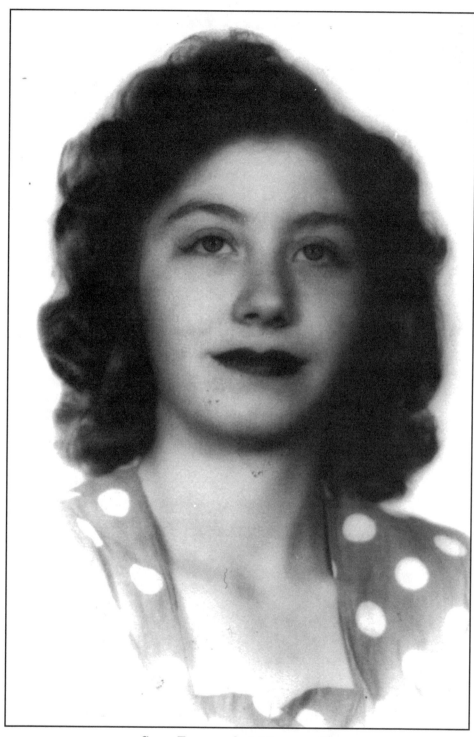

Snow Townsend at 17-years-old

Grandma Tressie Greene

Papaw Ralph Greene

Kim and TaRanda Greene in concert

Everette and Carolyn during their 40th Anniversary celebration

Tony working at his office

Daisy and Buck set up housekeeping

Tim and Brittany Greene

Brittany's baptism

The camping area at the Annual Gospel Singing Jubilee in Boone, NC

151

Carolyn and Everette in 2004

TaRanda and her mother, Mrs. Kiser, on her wedding day

Kim Greene's baptism

Tony and Tim's baptisms

TaRanda and Tony

After graduation, TaRanda poses with her paternal grandmother, Velma Kiser

While at the National Quartet Convention, TaRanda poses with Rex Nelon

Tony with Bill Gaither

TaRanda meets with Mr. and Mrs.
Glen Payne

Tim performs with Kirk Talley

TaRanda with Aaron and
Adam Crabb

Phil Naish, Tony and Ronnie
Brookshire

TaRanda with Michael
English

Michael Combs with Tim

CHAPTER NINE
JESUS IN ME

"It's just the Jesus in me, that makes
me believe, that there is victory for
every need."

— Tim Greene, "Jesus In Me," from
Whosoever Believes

Our days here on Earth are but a short season when compared to the glorious eternal existence that awaits those of us who have surrendered our lives to Jesus Christ.

For what is your life? It is even a vapour, that appeareth for a little time, and then vanisheth away. — James 4:14, KJV

In Heaven, there will be no pain, no anguish and no tragedies. God promises to wipe away all tears from our eyes. However, in this current world, no one owns a season pass to a pain-free existence.

The Greenes are no strangers to affliction and heartache, but in August of 2000, all their previous suffering would pale in comparison to that which was yet to come.

"It all started during the week of our Homecoming," Tim recalls. "I had never been so exhausted in my life — that's the only unusual thing I can remember about it. Then, after the Homecoming ended, I began sleeping twenty-two to twenty-three hours a day. After a few days of this, the family took me to the hospital for tests. At first, the diagnosis was Lyme disease from a tick bite, but the doctors didn't want to give me the treatment because they wanted to see if my immune system would just fight it off.

"After about two weeks of the abnormal sleeping, I started getting massive headaches. Well, the doctors then said I had spinal meningitis. I went through all the spinal taps and tests, but nothing they did helped. Then all the neurologists in Boone agreed that I had a brain virus — encephalitis. I figured that's what they tell you when they don't have a clue what's wrong with you.

"After nine or ten months of this, we didn't know where to turn. Then a friend told me he knew the head doctor of the Neuroscience Center at the University of North Carolina. The doctor told me to come down, that he felt they could help. So after going through the spinal taps, CT scans and MRIs all again, they decided they couldn't help. But they did suggest I see a psychiatrist, because they felt everything I was going through was just in my head. Well, they were right, the pain was in my head, but it was real and I wasn't making it up!

"So we started praying harder. Our family prayed, our church prayed, our friends prayed and the Southern Gospel community prayed. At that point, I had paralysis on my left side, and I could-

n't control the shaking. My legs began to hurt constantly, and it got to the place where I couldn't walk or get around at all.

"I had a friend from Atlanta who told me about Doctor Don Dennis, so I went down to see him. He was the first doctor who put a scope in my nose. After he looked into my sinus cavity, he backed up against the wall and said, 'My goodness, I've never seen anything like this before. You have mold all in your sinuses, and it is eating away at the bones and everything.'"

After much investigation, it turned out that the mold in his sinuses was the result of a faulty air-conditioner in Tim's car, which leaked water into the carpeting that eventually created significant mold growth, which, in turn, Tim constantly breathed in through the vents. Once the doctor knew what the problem was, he knew they had to move fast.

"He performed one major surgery, and then I went back every two weeks for more. He would have to scrape the cavity every visit. Well, it finally got to the point that I could no longer travel to Atlanta, so they admitted me to a hospital in Boone and another doctor conducted nine more surgeries. He did it once a week for nine weeks, putting me to sleep during the procedures.

"It was great to know what the problem was; it was even better getting treatment for it. A year later, I started getting a little better. I got to where I could walk again and things were beginning to look good, but the day after Christmas, I had an appointment with the doctor in Atlanta. He told me the only way that I would get better was to force my immune system to build antibodies against the mold.

"So, he gave me an allergy shot containing a small amount of the mold so my body would start fighting back naturally, and I immediately went into anaphylactic shock."

Anaphylactic shock is a serious allergic reaction. Symptoms could include dizziness, loss of consciousness, labored breathing, swelling of the tongue and breathing tubes, blueness of the skin, low blood pressure and heart failure.

"Reality hit me at that point," Tim's wife, Amy, said in tears. "When I lost my mother, it was hard. God was my strength, of course, but Tim was my emotional strength and helped me get through it. So, here I was with my emotional strength being taken away and possibly dying!"

"The emergency crews tried everything to get me through the reaction." Tim said. "After six hours, the doctor decided to cut the injection out of my arm. The reactions didn't stop, so he dug deeper and deeper into my arm until I had a two-and-a-half inch hole

all the way to the bone. They had to pack the hole every day for six months to get it to heal properly. This brought my system back down, putting me back in the bed without the ability to move my legs or move around.

"The doctor in Atlanta told us there was nothing else he could do and suggested I see a specialist in Dallas, Texas, at the Environmental Health Center. The facility specializes in getting people stabilized from severe allergy reactions. The doctor there didn't even want me to start testing immediately, as I had just done in Atlanta. He wanted to build up my immune system first, so he started me on a new diet and a lot of vitamins. He put me on IV's every other day, and I also had to sit in a dry-heat sauna to sweat the mold out of my system. And sure enough, it worked, thank the Lord."

"When we first got there, my dad and his wife, Betty, were there to help us get set up," Amy remembers. "We were heading for our room and ran into mold on the way there. Tim went into anaphylactic shock again right there on the stairwell. He couldn't even walk or feed himself when we had arrived there, so we were dragging him up to the room when it happened.

"But now, he was lying on the stairwell, dying before my eyes. Health care workers were trying to give him shots to stabilize him, and we tried everything to get him calmed down. It was at this point my world caved in. For the first time during his sickness, I thought Tim was going to die; and it was the first time that I gave all of it to God. When I did, that's when He began to do the work."

"On the seventh week in Dallas I was able to walk again, and after nine weeks I was back home," Tim recalls. "That was a miracle within itself because there are people out there right now that have gone through the same thing and never recovered. So I thank God for His hand in getting me back to normal."

Tim is not out of the woods yet. As of this writing, he still takes eight to sixteen shots a day and an IV once a week to continue building his immune system.

"If I have to live like this the rest of my life, it will still be great," Tim said. "The Lord has given me my legs and voice back. I'm able to be a husband and father again, and I'm again able to pastor and minister.

"I think the hardest part for me was watching my family suffer. Just hearing my daughter pray, 'Lord, please don't take my daddy.' Seeing the uncertainty on the faces of my wife, mother and granny was agonizing."

"We didn't know what the Lord was doing," Carolyn, Tim's mother, said. "We still don't know what He was doing, but we knew He was in control and He knew what He was doing. There were many sleepless nights and scary situations; many times, we didn't know if Tim was going to make it. I constantly worried about losing him. I thought it just doesn't seem right for parents to have to bury their children, and I remember praying, 'Lord, I can't take it anymore; I have to know, is he going to live or die?' The Lord spoke to me through Scripture with, 'Go thy way, thy son liveth (John 4:50),' and I knew from then on that Tim was going to be fine."

"God's grace helps you through your own suffering," Tim commented. "It's your concern for those you love that makes it hard. You hear preachers talk about it and you read about it in the Bible, but until you live it, you don't know what that experience is like. His grace is always sufficient; He's always faithful. And I'm living proof that He still performs miracles!"

"Through everything, Tim's faith never wavered," Carolyn said. "He would tell us, 'Even if I don't make it, I'm going to be the winner.' And he never gave any signs of giving up or doubting God."

"He had the faith of Job," Everette added. "It was his faith and encouragement that got the rest of us through it."

"That's probably the worst thing a parent ever has to go through," Carolyn said, "watching your children go through severe pain and suffering, and knowing there is nothing you can do to help."

"I have learned who God is through this," Tim said. "I'll never forget how much I learned about God and His grace while on my trip to Israel a few years ago. I looked for signs of Jesus while standing where He had stood preaching on the Mount of Olives. I had a new perspective of Him while standing where He fed the thousands with the two fishes and five loaves. All those sights blessed me, but it wasn't until I started getting sick that I learned He is without a doubt the Lily of the Valley. I learned it because I lived it; I saw it in Israel, but I lived it through the sickness.

"I have so much to be thankful for. The healing He performed in me was a miracle, but the greatest miracle was when He took my sins away when I was just a little boy. The greatest of all miracles is not healing me from my sickness; the greatest of all miracles is that He died for someone like me."

Tim's father, Everette, has had many health issues as well, and suffered multiple heart and breathing problems during the time of Tim's sickness. This only added to the stress and fatigue with everyone in the family.

"There was a period of maybe six months to a year that Tim couldn't even feed himself," Carolyn remembers. "So I was running back and forth between Everette and Tim, while Amy was gone to work. Then Amy would do the same when I was busy with things."

"There was a period of time where I couldn't do anything without help," Tim recalled. "Amy had to feed me, bathe me and clothe me. Because I couldn't take care of myself, this caused severe depression to set in on me. She would hold me when I cried and read to me when she thought I needed it. That also was hard for me: not being able to read my Bible. Amy knew when I needed it, and she would just pick up the Bible and come sit next to me and begin reading."

Tim and Amy's daughter, Brittany, suffered not only for what she saw her father go through, but also for what she watched her mother endure.

"Mom has always been the one to comfort me," she said, fighting back tears. "But if I ever came home from a bad day, Dad would tell me everything would be all right. But then when he got sick, he never did that — he couldn't.

"I remember hugging him, and he didn't respond; it was like hugging a dead man. It was the hardest thing I've ever had to deal with. I had a lot on my mind, but I couldn't talk with anyone because Mom had enough on hers, and my grandparents did, too, but watching my dad get worse was nearly more than I could bear.

"It hit me hard knowing that I might lose my daddy. It killed me not knowing if he would be there to walk me down the aisle one day — I just didn't know. I was scared that I was never going to see my Mom smile again. In a close family like ours, you can always spot a fake smile, and I could tell Mom was just trying to keep up appearances.

"We did everything to help relieve Dad's headaches, but nothing helped. I think one of the hardest things was when he asked me to tie a towel around his head to relieve the pain. I kept making it tighter and tighter, and he was screaming, 'Please get it tighter, please get it tighter.' I thought it was going to kill him. But nothing I did would help; he was just in so much pain. It scared me, because I had never seen anyone go through so much."

Of course, Tim's illness affected everyone in the family. Tony was no exception.

"Tony had a hard road during the whole time," Carolyn said. "He was trying to keep everything going with the ministry, the studio and the church."

"I don't see how he did it," Everette said. "I guess I would have been the first to throw up my hands and give in, but Tony never gave up."

"I think TaRanda was a great encouragement for him," Carolyn said. "She kept saying, 'We can do it; we can make it.' And I'm not sure he could have made it without her."

"It was definitely a time for maturity for Tony Greene," Danny Jones stated from his office at *The Singing News* headquarters in Boone. "It was the first time the whole ministry was placed solely on his shoulders, and thank God, TaRanda was there to help him bear the burden."

"Financially, Tony and TaRanda were there for us," a grateful Amy recalled, smiling. "Not one time while Tim was off the road did Tony allow Tim to go without a paycheck. Not once."

In fact, there were times when Tony brought a paycheck to Tim when there wasn't enough to pay himself or TaRanda — although when asked about it, at first, he tried to avoid the question.

"I promised Tim from the day he got sick, that if the Lord would help me, every Monday morning I would bring him a check." Tony said. "I mean, I had to take care of him — he's my brother — and he would have done the same for me."

Tony found that dealing with Tim's sickness was harder while he was away, on the road.

"Every night I would lie in my bunk when no one was around and weep my heart out," Tony said. Besides being brothers, Tim and Tony have always been inseparable best friends, too. "I'd cry

every single night; I would cry, pray and read my Bible. The hardest thing for me was not being able to do anything to help him.

"I would walk out on stage after stage and pulpit after pulpit, smiling — when deep down inside I didn't feel like smiling. Every night I made people laugh, when inside my heart I didn't really want to laugh. Night after night, I had to answer questions about Tim, and I began dreading interviews because I knew the subject would come up. I didn't want to think about it.

"I feel like the song we recorded recently that Phil Cross wrote, called 'Hold On,' was written just for us, because that is a song we have lived since August of 2000."

Tony and TaRanda shared that they were grateful that Tim was able to perform their wedding ceremony, although there were doubts that he'd make it through. Tim was so extremely weak and suffered such uncontrollable shaking that he had to be wheeled into the church to perform most of the ceremony from a wheelchair.

Tony said, "I really wondered if that was going to be the last time I'd ever see my brother alive."

"I think God has had a special way for us to live our songs," Tony said. "Starting August the thirteenth of the year 2000, we started learning what we had sung about all those years."

"It's true — we've learned the words to the songs we've been singing all our lives, but now we have learned the real meaning of the words," Tim said. "It's amazing how much more effective we can now be in the group's ministry. It's amazing how much more productive I can be as a preacher, teacher or pastor. And not just me, but my wife, Amy, as well."

"We can tell people that we understand what they are going through, and mean it," Amy said. "We can tell them we have walked in their shoes, and sometimes warn them about things they may see come about. Because of the strong pain medication the doctors prescribed for Tim, for example, I know what a drug addict and his wife must go through. Tim was not an addict, but when he needed to come off the pain medication, it was a horrible experience to go through.

"I know what it's like to have a sick spouse, and how it affects your marriage in every way. We know what it's like, so we can talk to people who are struggling with it day in and day out."

Tim added, "Not long ago, we were singing at a church where there was a little ten-year-old boy in a wheelchair in the audience." Tim said. "I'd given my testimony about how I'd been in a wheelchair for several months, and when I had come off the platform, he whispered for me to come over to him. I walked over and saw tears in his eyes. He said, 'You're the first person that's ever given me hope that I might walk again. Thank you.' And I thought if all my sickness was just to encourage that small child, then to God be the glory for it.

"It's like the words to a song the Lord gave me a while back: 'We don't have to know the reasons, and we don't have to know why; we just need to know that He knows what's best for us.'"

***

He must surely love me for the blessings I've received,
I have more than twenty men really
need;
But at times He must correct me on
the paths I wrongly take,
He unties my strongholds and my
heart He gently breaks.

He made His will, and He broke my
heart,
He received glory, and I fell apart;
But with love and compassion He lift-
ed me up,
He made His will, and He broke my
heart.

— By Tim Greene, "He Broke My Heart,"
Choral Favorites, Southern Gospel Style

CHAPTER TEN
HE'S NOT FINISHED WITH ME YET

"Forever, you are my Father. Forever,
on You I depend. Forever, or even
longer, forever my Friend"

— Tim Greene, "Forever,"
from *At the Cross*

The Greenes have built a ministry on harmonies that enter-
tain and lyrics that evangelize. Hit songs, popular albums and
videos dominate this award-winning trio's past; but more impor-
tantly, hundreds of thousands of lives have changed or been
touched because of their commitment to keeping God first.

The family literally grew up in the Southern Gospel industry
and has had many influences in their sound, presentation and
ministry. However, since the late seventies, the Greenes have
made their mark in the Gospel music arena and have influenced
others who came after them.

Besides the inspiring trio, the kids have an older brother
named Ronnie Brookshire who works behind the scenes in the
music industry. Ronnie and his lovely wife, Nancy, call Nashville,
Tennessee, their home, where Ronnie works as a record producer and studio engineer. In fact, Ronnie has produced and/or
engineered a few projects for the Greenes, as well as Michael W.
Smith, Sandi Patti, Whitney Houston, Babbie Mason, the
Martins, and others.

"When you listen to Southern Gospel trios today, you can't help but hear the influences of the Greenes' style in every mixed trio," Singing News editor Danny Jones said. "Every trio formed after the Greenes has adopted certain sounds and mannerisms from this one group of singers."

"I have never thought about that," Kim Greene remarked about that comment. "But I can only take that as a major compliment. Thinking about all the trios that have come along since the Greenes, I can see the influences and likenesses."

"Well, everyone has an idol or someone they look up to and want to be like," Everette commented. "I've had them and the children have had them; it's someone you grew up listening to or you looked up to. I think that is how the 'Greenes' sound' came about."

"When we first started, Tim's idol was Kenny Hinson," Carolyn

said. "Kim's idol was Reba Rambo, and Tony had several groups he wanted to sing like. It's flattering, and at the same time, it's humbling to know that now people want to be like you. I'm just thankful the Lord blessed our family with the talents they share, and cause people to want to sing, too."

"I think each of us had our own individual style," Kim explained. "And when you put those individual styles together, you get that particular sound. I don't think I could put my finger on what that sound is; I just know it when I hear it. That's something that I will listen for when around other trios now."

"I have noticed that, too," TaRanda said, nodding. "It's true; there isn't a singer in Southern Gospel music that has not been influenced in some way by this group I grew up listening to. I was one myself! I hear the 'Greenes' sound' in every group singing today."

"Well, that's humbling to hear," Tony said, as he smiled. "You know, I just hope if we ever hang our hat on the willow tree and say we're done, people will look back and say the Greenes did

their best to do it right. By no means have we been as successful as other groups, but I'm not sure how you measure success. To some artists, success is having twelve number-one songs or being on the Bill Gaither Homecoming Tour; to others it's how much money they are taking in each concert. I measure success by looking at how many people will be in Heaven that we helped win to the Lord.

"I think I heard it stated best by Billy Graham. Someone asked him how many millions he had led to the Lord, and he said, 'I won't know that until I get to Heaven, but I hope I've won at least one.' That's how we feel, too. We've always tried to make sure that everything we do is about the Lord and not about the Greenes.

"I think if we are judged by other people on the merits of just number one songs, or who gets the biggest paycheck, then I think we have been misjudged, because that's just not what we have tried to be. It has been our goal to do one thing: that is to encourage and win people to the Lord.

"When we get to Heaven, I don't think it's going to matter that we performed on a Bill Gaither video, or that we had a string of number ones. I don't think it will be of importance that we sang at the National Quartet Convention or Franklin Graham's Crusades. I think what will matter are the things we did in His name's sake when nobody else was looking — and that we won someone to Christ.

"It is important that in every concert we have a solemn moment and give people the opportunity to accept Jesus as Savior. It would be a tragedy to perform on stage and omit the most important and precious thing that there is — the opportunity to know Jesus personally as Lord.

"I think that a great number of ministries have missed the whole idea of what they are doing. Jesus told us to be fishers of men, and I think people today have gotten so caught up in the music that they have forgotten the most important thing — and that's to go fishing."

The Greenes have put ministry first in their career, and they are sensitive to what the Spirit wants. They minister to more than just fans and listeners; they also reach out to veteran singers and musicians as well. When spiritual siblings in the industry need prayer, they make sure their requests are on the Greenes' prayer list.

The songs the Greenes have written and recorded have blessed fans, listeners and veteran artists alike. Sometimes friends and artists find the strength to keep ministering after listening to a Greenes song or seeing them perform.

Although the group is moving close to celebrating thirty years in full-time ministry, they are still young enough for thirty or forty more. And their future seems bright; there are many ministry opportunities for this multitalented trio.

"I foresee the Greenes putting out songs that will minister to a

wide range of people," Tony said. "I think more and more our ministry is going to be focused around churches, because that's where our heart is. I see us, in the future, singing maybe two or three times a week. You know, for twenty-seven years, we have traveled four and five days a week. It's not the age with us — it's the miles. Tim and I like being at home more than ever before.

"I see us continuing to do more pastor's conferences, jubilees, revivals, and camp meetings, as well as our own services. I think we will start creating schedules more for when we want to do it, and when God wants us to do it, than how we've always done it before."

As mentioned earlier, Tim pastors Westview Baptist Church in Boone, and Tony is the music leader. They try to set their schedule so they will be able to be in their home church every Sunday, regardless of how difficult that commitment can sometimes be.

The Greenes also host their annual *Gospel Singing Jubilee Homecoming* each August at the High Country Fairgrounds in Boone, North Carolina. Thousands of fans from everywhere make their way to the scenic Appalachian Mountains to see the biggest names in Southern Gospel perform.

"We see fans come in from all over the United States," Tony

said. "We make the event ministry-oriented and have a great time every year. The artists we schedule to sing are anointed and always get the crowd on their feet, clapping their hands and praising God. Plus, we offer free camping facilities during the event. Everyone can come and have a great time."

"I always look forward to the Homecoming," TaRanda said, grinning. "We sing all week, but we're home the whole time. It is exciting to see God moving and blessing everyone in attendance; it's something everyone should experience."

"We have had so many great memories from past Homecomings," Tim said. "God has always shown up, and that's what it's all about."

"I guess nearly every artist who is singing professionally in Southern Gospel has performed at the Homecoming Jubilee," Tony said. "I have heard most of them say that the presence of God is so sweet at those events, that they just love being there."

"It's North Carolina's biggest Southern Gospel event," Everette said, "and it has grown so much from the early years. We have a lot of people who are in attendance every year. They come back year after year and have become our friends."

"Southern Gospel fans are the most loyal," Tony said. "They are always there for us in prayer and support us in ways that you would not believe. Our fans are our family, and we love them and miss them when we don't see them regularly."

"The fans are what keep us going sometimes, too," TaRanda

said. "The road gets tiresome and lonely, and just seeing those smiling faces at the concerts and churches helps keep our fires burning."

"The fans are just as much a part of our group as any other member," Tim adds. "I couldn't begin to tell you how many songs have been inspired by something a fan said or wrote in a letter. Their prayers have kept us safe on the road and their love has kept us in their hearts."

"And of course, the fans buy the records, tickets and videos so we can financially make it from week to week," Tony added. "They bless us financially and spiritually, and we're thankful for all they have done. We have, without a doubt, the best fans in the world. We don't take that for granted."

The fan base of the Greenes is ever expanding, and so is the number of family members. Tony and TaRanda are planning the arrival of their first child, which the preliminary ultrasound shows is a girl, in July 2004. They have decided to name her "Isabella Faith Greene," but "Buck" and "Daisy" are already referring to her as "Baby Belle".

Tony said that he and TaRanda originally made a pact once they discovered she was pregnant that if the baby were a boy, Tony would name him; if a girl, TaRanda would choose the name.

"At first I just knew we would have a boy. I wanted to name him 'Cooter Greene,' after Cooter on *The Dukes of Hazard*," he said, teasingly. "But, we found out the Lord is giving us a girl, so Daisy got to name her. We are both so happy about Baby Belle."

According to TaRanda, in spring 2004, they moved "out of [Tony's] bachelor pad, and into something that we can grow in" — just in time to fix up the nursery.

On their website, www.thegreenesgospel.com, TaRanda asked for prayer — not for herself, but, for Tony — during this period of time of waiting for the new arrival: "... not only is this his first baby, but I'm his first pregnant wife! I think my night sweats are

getting the best of him. He's sleeping with his pajamas, socks, and two extra blankets. He says he's getting tired of this 'not sleeping through the night' thing. I told him it's only the beginning!"

This being the first baby in the Greene family in ten years, needless to say, Baby Belle will get plenty of attention.

Who knows whether any or all of Tim's, Tony's, or Kim's children will follow in their talented family's footsteps. But as the Greenes' family tree continues to branch out, it will undoubtedly always remain rooted in the steadfast love for the Lord and for singing His praises for many generations to come.

***

Although the Lord Jesus continues to bless and work in the lives of the Greenes, the ministry still faces several important battles ahead. To give an idea of the life threatening struggles that still face the family, here are several excerpts from a letter, dated May 11, 2004, that Tim wrote to ministry supporters and fans:

Dear Friends:

My mold has come back in the form of candida. It's a type of yeast that grows from sugars and things you eat, so I am fasting for days trying to kill the mold, and I'd really appreciate your prayers. I wasn't able to be on the road from being sick and this weekend looks bleak, too. But maybe next week I can return, LORD willing. Dr. Dennis told me today the candida was going to kill me if I didn't do something. I don't know about that, but I know Someone who can do something, His name is JESUS. I have a swelling brain and paralysis in my left eye.

All can be reversed at a time later. We're praying it's soon.

This has been an ongoing battle and I know that GOD has a mighty plan for this trial — I just know it. I told our church last week that I believed that GOD would let me pastor 1,000 people by the year's end; I still believe that.

Don't look for me on the bus this week, but LORD willing, next. Nick Holland is doing an awesome job filling in for me. I hope he can put on a wig and sing Taranda's part when Baby Bell gets here. (haha)

Also, my brother Tony has suffered gout for years. He was born with only one kidney; now that kidney is failing. Besides being put on a donor list, there is a shot he can take monthly that will save the thirty-percent of the kidney that's working. He needs $3,000 each month for this shot. That's a lot of money. But he needs it.

Dad is doing some better. He is on dialysis every four days and he has diabetes, heart failure, and many other things wrong; but we're thanking GOD daily that he's still here and we thank God for every day we have him.

Westview Church is doing fantastic! We had a great revival with brother Phil Hoskins, the Freemans, and one night a young man gave his heart to JESUS. What more could you ask for?

May God Bless,
Tim Greene

Thankfully, Tim quickly recovered from this latest episode within a few weeks after composing the letter. And, as always, he takes a rather courageous and inspiring look at all of the trials he faces. He says that he sees Christ's tender mercy and workings, even during the time of the struggles that seem to surround the members of the group. He looks at these attacks through sensitive eyes of faith, relying upon the Heavenly Father for His strength.

Perhaps the Lord has allowed the Greenes to experience certain things so that they can better identify with others who are also hurting. Tim says that they have been through a lot, and that they now hope to be able to be there for the special people God sends their way. He added, "To this day, I have never questioned why I have to go through my own sickness. The only thing I ask is, 'Lord, how can You use this for Your glory?'

Tony downplays his own health issues and covers up his internal uncertainties through his legendary sense of humor. Although both brothers have concerns about the future, they have placed their complete confidence in the Master Physician, for the Bible promises that He is sufficient for every need and for every situation. "The Lord says He will never leave us or forsake us," Tony said. "I can rest in that. Period."

The Greenes have come to appreciate over the years that Romans 8:28 is certainly true, and that "all things work together for good to those who love God, to those who are the called according to His purpose."

That is not to say that all things are necessarily good; but our loving Christ promises that He can use all incidents — even bad circumstances in one's life — and make them work out for our ultimate growth and good. Through His love, He can take the worst situation, issue or hurt in a Christian's existence and ultimately bring goodness and beauty from it.

The Greenes often remember certain words written by the Apostle Paul to encourage his son in the faith, Timothy, such as in 2 Timothy 2:1, applying God's Word to their own circumstances: "You therefore, my son, be strong in the grace that is in Christ Jesus ... "

Through total confidence in the living Christ, Tim, TaRanda and Tony know that they can stand strong through His unmerited favor, regardless of the intensity of the storms of life. Their Anchor holds, and their ship is steady in spite of the changing winds of circumstance and the pounding waves of adversity.

"It's not the Greenes or our own abilities and might. For we have no real strength outside of Christ. It's all about Jesus, and reliance upon His power," Tim said. "His power, through the Holy Spirit, gives us the confidence to continue."

In the face of the many trials, burdens, and challenges that the family has faced over the years — regardless of the sufferings and testings that may await them in the future — they have found that the only key to real happiness, peace, and victory is found before the throne of Jesus, the true King of Kings and Lord of Lords.

"In all these years of singing, preaching, song-writing and

Kim, Karlye Jade, and Dean Hopper, and Tim, Amy and Brittany, and Tony and TaRanda Greene — *Photograph by Jonathan Burton Photography, Inc.*

working for the Savior, I've never one time asked for or wanted the applause of man, boy, girl or woman," Tim said a few years ago at a video taping of the *In His Eyes* video. "I've only wanted the Lord Jesus to be pleased."

Tim explained that it is the goal of the family that their ministry will glorify the loving Savior. Everything else is secondary. And with this, they feel that they have a charge to keep. "We want to tell others the precious story of His death, burial and resurrection, through song and words. It is through Jesus Christ that we can offer eternal hope to this sin-sick and dying world."

Besides of what the Greenes have personally endured, they also realize what others are going through at this particular period in time, too. Tony affirmed this in a December 2003 interview in *The Singing News*: "The past year, with all its challenges, has been one in which the group has really strived to make a year of encouragement. I've never seen the times like these in which we are living. People are discouraged, the economy is bad, and concert attendance has been down. All the artists have seen it. Money is tight, and many people are losing their jobs. Satan has used his unholy power to destroy in every possible way, and people just don't know what is going to happen. The Greenes as a family have taken the pulpit and shared the message of Isaiah 43:1—2: '... Fear not: for I have redeemed thee, I have called thee by thy name; thou art mine. When thou passest through the waters, I will be with thee...'

"That's our stronghold. This particular passage prepares us for these times in which we live and offers us comfort. We walk by faith and not by sight, and better days are ahead for the Children of God. I believe that's our message."

> ... Fear not: for I have redeemed thee,
> I have called thee by thy name; thou
> art mine. When thou passest through

the waters, I will be with thee; and
through the rivers, they shall not over-
flow thee: when thou walkest through
the fire, thou shalt not be burned; neither shall the flame kindle upon thee.

— Isaiah 43, KJV

Tony recently summed up the family's viewpoint at a concert
at a small, out-of-the-way country church in Harts, West
Virginia, when he spoke to the congregation, "Folks, the Greene
family is really no different than anyone here this evening. We all
have our own difficulties and sufferings in this life, don't we? But
if you and I know Jesus, we have Someone who recognizes our
needs and is touched by our infirmities, heartaches, and concerns.

"When we cry out to Jesus, He draws close to us. When some of
life's most difficult, unplanned circumstances come and we are
tempted to give up the fight, or when it seems that all hope is
gone, and in comes those nagging doubts, there is only one thing
that you and I can do — 'hold on!'"

HOLD ON

When there's no steps to take,
No moves left to make,
Oppressing fears, tormenting doubts,
Prayer and prayer, still there's no way
out,
And it seems like pain is all you gain.

Hold on, hold on,
Through every storm, hold on.
Even in the darkest night,
Walk by faith and not by sight.
Hold on, hold on.

There's a Father of love,
Hold peace like a dove,
In the midst of all your dark despair
With open arms He's waiting there.
To hold you 'til the hurt is gone.

Hold on, hold on
Through every storm hold on.
Even in the darkest night,
Walk by faith and not by sight.
Hold on, hold on.†

THE END

THE AUTHOR WISHES TO THANK:

With any book, you will find many people behind the scenes who make a project possible—this book is no different. Many talented individuals made this project possible, and I want you, the reader, to know their names. It's my job as a writer to put thoughts and feelings into sentences and chapters. Yet, I find myself searching for suitable words when describing my appreciation for those who've helped — people like Bill Gaither for taking the time to write such a poignant foreword.

The family and friends of the Greene family, including Tim, Tony and TaRanda, Everette and Carolyn Greene, Kim Greene Hopper, Amy and Brittany Greene, Snow Townsend, Tressie Greene and Donna Cook.

I also want to thank Keith and Cheryl Davis, Tim and Renee Fortune at Woodland Press/Woodland Gospel for their partnership and friendship. I especially want to thank Cheryl, whose editing skills remind me of the Blood of Christ—having covered a multitude of sins.

I would like to offer a special thank you to Maurice Templeton, Danny Jones and the whole staff at the Singing News Magazine (www.singingnews.com) for making their facilities and archives available during this project.

I would also like to thank Dottie Rambo, Amy Lambert Templeton, Milena Parks, Allison Stinson, Melanie Kocolowski, Ray Flynn, Riley Joe Evans, Paul and Shelia Heil, Phil Cross, Calvin Ray Evans and Jerry Stock for significant contributions to this project. — *Mike Collins*

***

Woodland Gospel Publishing note: We would like to express our sincere gratitude to the Greene family for their kindness and cooperation in making this biography a reality. This lovely family has won our hearts and our admiration during the time we have gotten to know them. They have shown themselves to be genuine in every way. They live what they believe, and they are quick to give Christ all credit and glory for years of successful ministry.

We also thank Mike Collins and all who contributed to this project.

Above all things, we thank the Lord Jesus Christ for His grace and guidance in this company. Lord, may everything we do as a book-publishing firm be pleasing in Your sight.

† "Hold On," written by Phil Cross, used by permission. "Hold On," recorded by The Greenes, is available on their *Whosoever Believes* CD album.

GOOD NEWS

Jesus has paid the price for you on Calvary. Now it is up to you to accept what He has done for you by faith. You need to understand that.....

1. God loves you.

"For God so loved the world that He gave His only begotten Son, that whosoever believeth in Him should not perish, but have everlasting life. For God sent not His Son into the world to condemn the world, but that the world through Him might be saved." (John 3:16-17)

"God demonstrates His own love toward us, in that while we were yet sinners, Christ died for us." (Romans 5:8)

2. Man is a sinner, separated from God

"For all have sinned and come short of the glory of God." (Romans 3:23)

"For the wages of sin is death; but the gift of God is eternal life through Jesus Christ our Lord." (Romans 6:23).

3. Jesus is the only way to God

"Neither is there salvation in any other: for there is none other name under heaven given among men, whereby we must be saved." (Acts 4:12)

"Jesus said to him, 'I am the way, the truth and the life. No one comes to the Father except through me.'" (John 14:6)

4. You must receive Jesus as Lord and Savior

"Except a man be born again, he cannot see the kingdom of God" (John 3:3)

"That is thou shalt confess with thy mouth the Lord Jesus, and shalt believe in thine heart that God hath raised him from the dead, thou shalt be saved. For whosoever shall call upon the name of the Lord shall be saved." (Romans 10:9,13)

Do you feel the Spirit of God touching your heart right now in a special way? Do you feel Him drawing you to Him? If you do, don't turn Him away. The Bible says, "Behold, now is the accepted time; behold, now is the day of salvation." (2 Corinthians 6:2).

Perhaps you would like to pray this prayer from the bottom of your heart.

Dear Jesus, I know I am a sinner. I know that you died on the cross for my sins, was buried in a borrowed tomb, and rose from the dead. I open my heart to receive You as my Savior and Lord. Forgive me of my sins. Change me, and make me into the kind of person You want me to be. Help me to live for You and to share Your love with others for all the days of my life. Amen.

***

CONTACT FORM

If you invited Jesus Christ into your heart while reading *Hold On*, or you are inspired and want to know more about the Savior, contact the Greenes.

The Greenes
PO Box 446 DTS
Boone, NC 28607

Also, if you would like to write Woodland Gospel, we will send you additional information to help you as you begin this wonderful, exciting new life in Him.

I recently accepted Christ as my personal Savior. Please send me free literature to assist me in my Christian walk.

NAME _____

ADDRESS _____

STATE _____ ZIP _____

E-mail _____

Send this form to:
Woodland Gospel Publishing
118 Woodland Drive, Suite 1101
Chapmanville, WV 25508
Congratulations on your decision to follow Jesus.
Please allow several weeks to receive your packet.

To personally contact the Greenes for bookings, or to order additional copies of *Hold On: The Authorized Biography of The Greenes*, you can send your correspondence to:

The Greenes
PO Box 446 DTS
Boone, NC 28607

www.thegreenesgospel.com

Email
tim@thegreenesgospel.com
taranda@thegreenesgospel.com
tony@thegreenesgospel.com
customerservice@thegreenesgospel.com

Published In Beautiful West Virginia By

WOODLAND GOSPEL PUBLISHING HOUSE

A Division Of Woodland Press, LLC

See Our Other Great Titles:
www.woodlandgospel.com
(304) 752-7500

info@woodlandgospel.com